Silent Warfare

Managing Nuclear Chemical Biological (WMD) Disasters

Silent Warfare

Managing Nuclear Chemical Biological (WMD) Disasters

Brig (Dr) H K Kar
MSc, M Tech, FIE, FINP, PhD

Manas Publications
New Delhi - 110 002 (India)

MANAS PUBLICATIONS
(We Convert Fighters into Writers)
(Publishers, Library Suppliers, Importers & Exporters)
4402/5-A, Ansari Road (Opp. HDFC Bank)
Darya Ganj, New Delhi-110 002 (India)
Off. (23260783, 23265523, Fax: 011-23272766
E-mail: manaspublications@vsnl.com
manaspublications@gmail.com

ISBN 81-7049-180-0
₹ 495/-

Designed at

Manas Publications

Printed in India at
Harmain Offsets, Delhi
and published by Mrs Suman Lata for
Manas Publications, 4402/5-A,
Ansari Road, (Opp. HDFC Bank),
Darya Ganj, New Delhi-110 002 (INDIA)

Preface

Would the attack on the Twin Towers in New York, with aircraft commandeered by Islamic fundamentalist suicide attackers be considered an attack with Weapons of Mass Destruction (WMD)? Was it the beginning of the awareness of the effects of WMD on civilized society? Or did the awareness start germinating after the sarin gas attack incident in the Tokyo subway by the Aum Shinrikyo cult in the mid-nineties, that killed a dozen people, seriously injured over fifty more, and mildly injured nearly one thousand persons? WMD include any weapon or device that are intended or have the capability, to cause death or serious injury, to a significant number of people through the release of poisonous or toxic chemicals or their precursors, disease organism or radiation or radioactivity.

With the advanced technology available in the industries of many countries and/or the funds available to purchase through overt or covert means from certain countries, easy access to WMD has become a reality. These could be nuclear, radiological, chemical or biological weapons. Some devices can be manufactured using simple chemical processes known to any university student. Who will use them, when, how and where are the only questions that remain.

Use of WMD by a country against another would, under normal circumstances not take place unless there is a war or aggression by a country on another. However, the networked and interdependent nature of developed society offers non-state actors like terrorists a perfect target for radiological, chemical or biological WMD. There are three factors that make us vulnerable to WMD. The first is the manner in which complex technology in our society can be turned against itself by the terrorists. For example, a ballpoint pen factory can be the source of a chemical weapon. 'X' chemical added to the ink in the refill material of a ballpoint pen can produce the deadly mustard gas. The second is the suicide mission or "Jehad", where there is no requirement for the terrorists to have an escape plan, which implies that entry to the target area is the only problem. The third is that the terrorists aim for attention appears to have changed to the desire to kill perceived enemies in greater numbers.

The National Disaster Management Plan prepared by the High Powered Committee chaired by Shri JC Pant focused basically against natural disasters and to a limited extent to cover man-made disasters like chemical, industrial and disasters in nuclear installations. However, management of WMD disasters caused by terrorists or non-state actors has not been included in its purview. The report published in the two volumes has presumably been circulated to all concerned down to district level in all states of India. However, during a Workshop on Disaster Management which I attended in the Centre for Disaster Management, New Delhi, alongwith District Collectors, District Magistrates, Police Officers, Fire Fighting Officers etc, it transpired that most of the participants were unaware of these two volumes, published after two years of effort by a high level study group. The general consensus was that the volumes of the report might have been received in their respective departments, and might have been locked up in the almirahs in their offices and may be gathering dust.

A major objective of this book is to stress the nature and magnitude of disasters that could take place because of the use of WMD, the state of awareness and preparedness that we as a nation have against WMD disasters and provide grass-root basic methods to mitigate such disasters. I have tried to write this book in a reader friendly manner, avoiding complicated technical aspects as far as possible, so that the general public reads it, and concerned authorities adopt the operating procedures. Since the organisations recommended for disaster management in the Disaster Management Plan are at various stages of formation, I have only recommended incorporation of specialised Rapid Reaction Teams in the organisations to be. Hopefully, when these organisations take shape on ground, some of the recommendations made by me will be accommodated, albeit with modifications as deemed necessary. **Unfortunately, it is unlikely that the importance of WMD disaster management will be understood till a WMD disaster actually takes place in our country.**

This book is an attempt to spread the awareness of WMD disasters and their mitigation among the general public and government officials, so that alternatives are available to planners and decision-makers of disaster management policy and plans. The management techniques recommended in this book have evolved out of personal visualisation of WMD disasters and discussion with colleagues dealing with the subject, as well as from review of related literature. The book is laid out in nine chapters and appendices covering various aspects of preparation for WMD disasters and their mitigation.

Chapter 1 tries to depict a chemical disaster scenario that takes place in a market area in New Delhi, on **20 May 2006**, and portrays the sequence of action that would be taking place, assuming that the nation has been taking positive steps in implementing various recommendations in preparation of mitigating WMD disasters.

Chapter 2 discusses the necessity of a National Disaster Management Plan. It tabulates the nuances of WMD disasters, analyses the approach to WMD disasters in USA and recommends the creation of Rapid Reaction Teams (RRT) which should be dovetailed into the organisations that are likely to be created as part of the National Disaster Management Plan. This would help to guide planners to make use of and develop the existing wheels instead of trying to re-invent issues. The chapter also briefly dwells upon the preparations necessary and response required at the level of the district, state and centre to mitigate the disasters due to WMD.

Chapter 3 analyses the security environment and in relation to WMD suggests, that the possibility of use (or misuse) of WMD by terrorists and non-state actors is high.

Chapter 4 analyses the various ways in which a chemical disaster could take place and briefly describes the salient characteristics of chemical agents. It also describes a chemical disaster scenario, and discusses the manner in which the various agencies involved in mitigating a chemical disaster such as the police, military, medical authorities, fire department, civil defence organisation, NGOs, media and the district administration, would be required to act.

The chapter analyses in detail the sequence of mitigation in a disaster area and summarises the tasks of the various organisations.

Chapter 5 discusses the likely effects of a nuclear disaster and radiological fallout and recommends steps to mitigate them. The duties that various agencies could be ascribed to are discussed.

Chapter 6 attempts to bring out the nuances of biological agents and the possibility of their becoming weapons of choice by terrorists. The characteristics of biological agents and the mitigation procedures to be adopted by various agencies have also been discussed in this chapter.

Chapter 7 suggests that awareness of WMD disasters is essential among the general public without giving rise to panic. The chapter discusses the preparations that common people could do to cater for emergencies as well as the immediate actions to be taken in case of nuclear, chemical and radiological disaster.

Chapter 8 recommends simple preparations to be undertaken by hospitals so that they are in a position to handle mass casualties contaminated by nuclear radiation, chemical or biological agents.

Chapter 9 attempts to highlight the important proceedings of the previous chapters and summarises the important recommendations so that WMD disasters do not take the general public and government organisations by surprise, and the nation is in a position to react to such disasters effectively and efficiently.

Although this book has been written somewhat in an India-centric perspective, the visualisation of the WMD disasters and their mitigation would be universally acceptable and the preparation or mitigation techniques could be considered for implementation not only in India, but also in countries faced with the menace of terrorism. Since terrorism has become a global phenomenon, the peremptory measures for mitigation of WMD disasters could also be recognised globally.

Brig (Dr) H.K. Kar

Acknowledgements

This book has been written with the intellectual advice and criticism of many of my professional colleagues and a large number of constructs have been the result of serious discussions on the subject over a period of time. It is both a pleasure and duty to express my gratitude to all those who, in one way or another, have helped me in this arduous and mind-searching task.

The first and the last nuclear bomb exploded on humanity in 1945. There have been many instances of chemical attacks since then, but not very much detail is readily available except in news items. Biological disasters, if any, are so shrouded in politics that very little is recorded in uncensored publications. Therefore, in writing a book of this nature one has to depend per force on the recorded wisdom of specialists in the field of NBC warfare.

As Deputy Director General, NBC Warfare, in the Army Headquarters (India), I have been attending and participating in numerous lectures, workshops and seminars on the subject. During these occasions, I have been collecting material for my future study and analyses, little realising that I would like to put down my learnings in the form of a book and make use of this invaluable material. Quite a few photographs, tables etc. that I have used in this book, were collected by me while attending these seminars and workshops and I never felt the necessity of enquiring about the sources at that point of time. I would therefore like to humbly acknowledge with gratitude, the wisdom of the persons whose permission I have not been able to obtain prior to including their knowledge in my book and sincerely hope that they will appreciate this possible inadvertent lapse, rather than take offence. Information available on the Internet was also very helpful. Needless to say, I assume full responsibility for the many shortcomings of the book.

I owe special thanks to Brig S.K. Sharma who has been a constant source of support and encouragement and edited the first draft. I am grateful to Brig A.K. Pathak for offering valuable comments to refine the subject matter. My thanks to Nb Sub Pattanaik and Mrs Kiran for typing the manuscript in its various stages and preparing the tables and figures. I also wish to thank Mr. Vivek Garg (the publisher) for his patience, guidance and encouragement.

Last but not the least, my sincere thanks to my wife Mithu and our children Abhik, Pratik and Samhita, but for whose inspiration and continuous encouragement, I may not have had the perseverance to complete "Silent Warfare"

Brig (Dr) H.K. Kar

Contents

Abbreviations

ACADA	Automatic Chemical Agent Detection and Alarm system
BTT	Break Through Time
BTWC	Biological and Toxins Weapons Convention
CAM	Chemical Agent Monitor
CISF	Central Industrial Security Force
CWC	Chemical Weapons Convention
FBI	Federal Bureau of Investigation
FEMA	Federal Emergency Management Agency
GOC	General Officer Commanding
GZ	Ground Zero
HAZMAT	Hazardous Materials
ITBP	Indo Tibetan Border Police
NBC	Nuclear Biological Chemical
NDMA	National Disaster Management Authority
OC	Officer Commanding
RAD	Radiation Absorbed Dose
RAID	Rapid Assessment and Initial Detection Element

RRT	Rapid Reaction Team
RVD	Residual Vapour Detector
SARS	Severe Acute Respiratory Syndrome
SOP	Standard Operating Procedure
TCDP	Three Colour Detector Paper
WMD	Weapons of Mass Destruction

Glossary

Automatic Chemical Agent Detection and Alarm (ACADA) System detects nerve and mustard agents and sets out an alarm on detection of the chemical agent so that the personnel can quickly put on the respirator and take necessary precautions. It is generally mounted on a vehicle.

Break Through Time (BTT) is the time required for a chemical to penetrate through any material.

Canister is fitted on to the respirator for breathing. Due to the filters in the canister breathing resistance occurs. A canister can be used in a contaminated environment for two hours, after which it has to be replaced.

Casualty Bag Full is used to carry lying casualty from contaminated area. It has a charcoal lining and prevents contamination of neighbouring personnel while being transported.

Casualty Bag Half covers the individual from waist upwards only. It is used by contaminated casualties who can walk. This prevents them from contaminating others while proceeding for medical assistance.

Chemical Agent Monitor (CAM) is a hand-held instrument used for detecting mustard and nerve agents. It can be used to mark contaminated zone, check contaminated vehicles and personnel etc.

Decontamination suit is an impermeable suit made of rubber. It is used by the decontamination teams to prevent ingress of contaminated water while conducting decontamination. It does not protect against chemical agents.

Dose Rate is the rate at which radiation is received, expressed in roentgens per hour.

Gloves consist of an outer cover of neoprene rubber that provides protection against chemical contamination for twenty-four hours. It also has a set of inner gloves made of cotton to provide comfort and absorb sweat.

Ground Zero is the point on the ground surface vertically beneath or above which a nuclear device has exploded. The greatest damage of all kinds occurs here.

Individual Chemical Agent Detector (ICAD) has the capability to detect simultaneously nerve, blister, blood and choking agents. It warns through both audio and visual alarm. It is light in weight (200 gm) and is carried by personnel operating near likely chemically contaminated areas.

Kiloton is the power of a nuclear weapon and is expressed in terms of the total energy released by trinitrotoluene (TNT) when it explodes. Thus a one kiloton nuclear bomb is one which releases the same amount of energy as the explosion of one kiloton (1000 tons) of TNT. A 20 kiloton weapon is referred to as a nominal yield atomic weapon.

NBC Suit Permeable permits air to pass through to reduce heat stress while it prevents chemicals to break through for a particular period of time, generally six hours. The suit has an outer layer of permeable wicking type material and inner layer of activated charcoal and muslin. It provides protection against chemical contamination and residual nuclear hazard.

Overboots are made of butyl rubber and worn over normal shoes. The left and right foot of the overboot is interchangeable. The overboots have a life of about twenty-four hours in a contaminated environment.

Pocket Type Dosimeter is used to measure radiation dose and dose rate in the environment, and can be carried by an individual. It has a range of 0-1000 Rads.

Radiation Dose is the amount of nuclear radiation energy absorbed by a person and is measured in Rads (Radiation abosrbed dose).

Residual Vapour Detector (RVD) kit is capable of detecting residual chemical warfare agents present in the air. The kit contains a sampling pump and sealed glass detector tubes. The change of colour of reagent inside the tube indicates the presence of specific toxic agents in the air. The kit can detect nerve agents, sulphur mustard, cyanogen chloride, hydrogen cyanide and phosgene.

Respirator provides respiratory protection against chemical and biological agents and radioactive dust. It is made of butyl rubber and is worn over the face. It has a pneumatic sealing for comfort and eyepieces for good vision. Condensation over the eyepieces is kept to the minimum by routing incoming air over them.

Resuscitator is used for giving artificial respiration to casualties. These can be manually or electrically operated.

Three-Coloured Detector Paper (TCDP) is provided in the form of a booklet containing 10 pages. The detector paper is peeled off from the booklet and attached to any surface. Appearance of colour spots confirms presence of chemical warfare agent. The agent is identified as per the colour chart provided with the booklet.

Watch Type Dosimeter is made in the shape of a watch and worn around the wrist by individuals. It detects gamma radiations and neutrons and gives the cumulative dose absorbed by an individual. It does not display the radiation absorbed and a specific reader is required to read the dose.

List of Figures

List of Tables

1

20 May 2006—New Delhi

5.00 p.m. New Delhi

The Chairman of National Disaster Management Authority (NDMA) was in a reflective mood as he entered his car to go back to his office in the North Block. As he drove through the busy streets of Delhi from Vigyan Bhawan, he thought over the proceedings of the Quarterly Interaction Seminar on Disaster Management, which had been going on there for the past two days. The attendance was far better than on the previous occasion. The General Officer Commanding (GOC) Delhi Area, Major General Pratik Oberoi; Mr Dipak Dixit, I.G.Police; Mr. Shibdas Nandi, Director General Civil Defence; Dr Samhita Sharma, Secretary of State Health Ministry; Mr Dilip Das, Chief Fire Officer; Mrs. Padmaja Srivastav from CARE (an NGO) were present among others. The representation from the States was also good. Mr. Abhik Kar, Chairman of NDMA was contented with the progress made in the past two years in preparing to mitigate disasters in the country. The efforts made by the various agencies, particularly in preparation to face Weapons of Mass Destruction Disasters was commendable. As he entered his office in the North Block, his personal assistant informed him that the Chief Minister, Delhi, had called and requested to be called back urgently. He looked at the clock it was **5.25 p.m.,** he asked his personal assistant to connect him to the Chief Minister who was also a personal friend.

5.00 p.m. North Extension Market

Mr. Rajat Chadda was looking out of the verandah of his sixth floor flat in North Extension Market, seeing the shoppers build-up in the market area. He was looking forward to a brisk sale this evening in his departmental store in the market below. After all, a Friday evening is as good as a weekend in Delhi where Saturdays and Sundays are holidays in all Government offices. Suddenly he noticed a young boy about ten years of age falling down near the litter bin after throwing an empty paper packet into it. As he got up and tried to move, he shuddered and fell down again. People around him approached to help; but they too did not seem to be in a fit state. Mr Chadda was indeed concerned, but was not sure as to what to do. He could see the commotion building up, but could not make out as to what exactly was going on. Could it be the indications of an outbreak of yet another disease or maybe chemical leak? He looked towards the area below him once again; this time with a more focused thought. Yes, he could observe a few people holding their handkerchiefs to their faces as they tried to cross that area. Soon, a pandemonium broke out. People rushing out of the air-conditioned market in the area and collapsing on the pavement, cars taking off from the parking area and banging into other cars creating traffic blockade. Mr Chadda, a voluntary member of the local Civil Defence Organisation, wasted no time. He picked up his telephone, and called 100....

5.05 p.m. Police Station Chanakyapuri

Inspector Shyam Singh was cheerful on the cool and peaceful day and was planning to go early so that he could take his family for an evening out. This week had been busy with security arrangements for VIPs; in fact he had no time even to buy the textbooks for his children. As the telephone rang he hoped that it would not be an emergency call. However, what Mr. Rajat Chadda had to tell him was much more than an usual emergency. It was in fact a disaster in the making.

5.05 p.m. North Extension Market

Sub-Inspector Rajesh Singh was relaxing in the police control van in North Extension area. Only the driver was with him; the four policemen in the van had gone on their beat around the market. The pickpockets and bag snatchers in the market had become experts to disappear after an operation, thus bringing a bad name to the police. Suddenly he saw Sukhpal Singh stumbling towards the police van, his eyes and nose watering. With great difficulty he could report to him about some chemical leak in the market and collapsed; he could not give any details. He asked the driver to take out the NBC protective sets, called up the Police Headquarters and started to attend to Sukhpal Singh. His sixth sense worked and he froze in his tracks; this was a case of chemical contamination that could attack him also if he was not cautious. He quickly donned the NBC protective gear and washed the face of Sukhpal with water. He knew what his duty was and rushed to the market donning his protective gear.

5.05 p.m. Police Headquarters Chanakyapuri

There was a sudden flurry of activities as the message of a likely disaster in North Extension Market was received at the emergency number 100. The person had identified himself as Major Rajat Chadda (retired) and hence the report could be authentic. This was immediately followed by a radio message from Sub-Inspector Rajesh Singh who informed him about Sukhpal Singh's report and condition and said that he would be moving to the affected area for a first-hand report of what was going on. The officer on duty immediately contacted the DIG Police, Delhi Cantonment Area and informed him of the occurrence of the disaster. He simultaneously informed all the mobile police posts of the incident and ordered them to be on standby for further orders. He also deputed an officer to contact the District Collector, Military Station Commander, District Medical Officer, District Fire Officer, Civil Defence Officer and the other concerned personnel listed in the Disaster Management Standard Operating Procedure (SOP) and inform them of the incident.

5.10 p.m. Africa Avenue

Major General Pratik Oberoi was on his way home from Vigyan Bhawan when he received an emergency call on the radio set from DIG Police, Delhi Cantonment. It seemed an attack by terrorists had taken place in North Extension Market area near the I.T Park. The GOC immediately rang up his headquarters and directed the 'Order' Group to assemble at the Area Headquarters Conference Room immediately, since a chemical attack by terrorists had possibly taken place. He also ordered for a small reconnaissance party with NBC protective gears to visit the area of the incident and give a situation report on his cellphone at the earliest.

5.10 p.m. Karol Bagh

The District Magistrate's office was in a state of utter chaos. The shopkeepers of Dhaula Kuan area demanded justice, while Mr Promod Datta, the young and dynamic District Magistrate, was locked up in his office discussing the issue with their leaders to find a viable solution. It was impossible for the office assistant to put the District Magistrate through on telephone to the DIG Police, Cantonment Area. The office assistant pushed his way through into the conference room, much to the annoyance of the public leaders and told Mr Datta of the DIG's urgent call. Mr Datta rang up the DIG himself. It did not take time for him to understand what had hit his area of responsibility. He was immediately on his feet, and explaining to the leaders about the emergency situation called off the meeting for the day. He rushed out of his office, informed the demonstrators of the emergency and requested them to help him mitigate the situation. He was aware that he could not do much on ground unless he had the NBC protective gear. Unfortunately, he had not been able to convince the local government of the need to procure NBC protective gears, and now he was in a hapless situation. Thanks to golf, the Military Station Commander and he had become good friends, and he was confident that he could depend on the army. He spoke to the Station Commander on telephone and came to know that he had already sent a reconnaissance party to the site. He thanked him, for having sent the troops without getting into the protocol of formal requisition. Thereafter, he formally requisitioned the assistance of the Army (verbally) and said that he would be sending the same in writing immediately. He also requested the Station Commander to give him twenty sets of protective equipment so that he could go and set up the Control Headquarters at site. Brigadier Dixit was happy to hear the concern of Mr. Datta and his initiative to set up the Control Headquarters, and promised all help to the District Administration. They agreed to keep in touch... He then ordered the Rapid Reaction Team of the police located at Karol Bagh Fire Station to move to the disaster site at the earliest.

5:15 p.m. Police Headquarters Delhi Cantonment

The DIG Delhi Cantonment area quickly assessed the type of disaster (being qualified in Disaster Management course) and guessed that it was a chemical attack, though the magnitude of the disaster was not known to him. He contacted the IG Police, GOC Delhi Area Headquarters and the District Magistrate, and informed them of the disaster. He also took this opportunity to speak to the Home Minister directly and informed him of the disaster, though he could not give any details. Silently he took credit for being the first person to report to the Minister. He then made sure that the officers in the police headquarters were detailed to intimate all concerned as per the SOP about the disaster. He then took the initiative to take over charge of the situation and rushed to the North Extension Market.

5:15 p.m. Police Control Vans North Delhi

The police control vans having received the message of the chemical disaster took out the NBC protective gears from their hermetically sealed packings and checked that the respirators were fitting snugly on to their faces. They also rehearsed fitting the canisters on to the respirators. They were tense indeed while awaiting further orders. The orders which came in were to establish road blocks on the roads approaching/leaving the affected area by **6.00 p.m.**

- Police control vehicles 4075, 5088, 9504 and 2569 were to home onto the Netaji Subhash Marg and Chanakya Marg crossing and divert all vehicles moving towards North Extension Market. They were also to ensure as far as possible to advise people not to exit beyond that point.
- Similarly five police control vans were directed to the crossing of Satya Marg and Africa Avenue and some vehicles to the intersection of Broad Street and Joshi Road.
- The task was to prevent vehicles from going into the North Extension Market beyond the checkpoints and also to prevent vehicles and personnel to go out of the checkpoints (so that the contaminated vehicles and persons do not further contaminate the environment).

5.15 p.m. 258 Bomb Disposal Company, Delhi Cantonment

Major Abhishek Sharma, the Officer Commanding of 258 Bomb Disposal Company located at Delhi was cheering his company team playing a basketball match with the Dogra Battalion. In fact the entire company was in the basketball ground cheering their team. Suddenly, the Subedar Major brought a jawan who reported that the duty clerk had received a message directly from the GOC Delhi Area, for him (Officer Commanding) to speak to the GOC Delhi Area immediately. As he called up the GOC on his cell phone he received the news of the incident and was called to the Area Headquarters. He briefed his Second in Command Captain Alok Dutta and his Subedar Major to prepare the men and await further orders from him. He then proceeded to the Area Headquarters.

5.20 p.m. Headquarters 62 Field Ambulance, Delhi Cantonment

Major Ravi Reddy, the officiating Commanding Officer of 62 Field Ambulance, was visiting the unit, which was preparing for the forthcoming administrative inspection. As he reached his office the duty clerk buzzed on the intercom and informed him that the GOC Delhi Area was on line. The GOC informed him of the probable disaster and asked him to move to the Area Headquarters immediately. Major Reddy called Captain Negi who was nearby and told him about the disaster. He ordered him to prepare the medical team and await further orders.

5.30 p.m. Nirman Bhawan

The Emergency Medical Relief Director of Delhi was contacted by the Police Control Headquarters as per the SOP by **5.15 p.m.** However, the Director had difficulty in contacting the Emergency Wings of the hospitals on telephone. They seemed to be constantly engaged. He also had difficulty in tracing the Registrars of the concerned hospitals. They had left their offices and were yet to reach home. He kept working on the telephone from his office and gave the directions to the hospitals to gear up as per SOP, to receive and treat the casualties. He telephoned the Commandant, Army Base Hospital, and requested him to receive the first lot of casualties while the civil hospitals geared up. He was confident that the Army hospital would be ready in a quicker timeframe than the civil hospitals, with the facilities required in the **Contaminated Area** and segregation of the hospital in the **Clean Area.**

5.35 p.m. Station Headquarters Delhi Cantonment

The Order Group of Delhi Area was being briefed. They were informed that Major Ajay Singh of 4 JAT Infantry Battalion and a reconnaissance team had already proceeded to the area of the disaster and would be giving a clear picture of the disaster shortly. GOC Delhi Area (who had coincidentally returned from the two-day seminar on Disaster Management) also present in the briefing explained the arrangements being planned by the local Government to mitigate the disaster. Directions were also given to obtain clearance from Military Operations Directorate for issue of NBC protective equipment. The following directions were given to the Order Group:

- The Field Ambulance to move the medical team to the Bomb Disposal Unit by **6.15 p.m.**
- The Bomb Disposal Company to move the response team into the area of disaster by **6.40 p.m.**
- The 4 JAT Infantry Battalion to prepare a column of two hundred personnel to move to the area of disaster and await further orders. No Move Before (nmb) **7.00 p.m.** This party should be administratively prepared to work through the night in the disaster area. The column should be in possession of NBC protective gears.

- The Base Hospital to prepare the premises as per existing Disaster Management Plan to receive at least four hundred contaminated casualties. The Hospital should be prepared to receive the causalties latest by **6.45 p.m.**, if not earlier.
- The Field Ambulance to muster up as many ambulances as possible from the Base Hospital as well as other units and send them to report to the Bomb Disposal Company as early as possible. The crews of the ambulances were to carry their NBC protective gears with them. If they did not have adequate number of protective sets, then the same were to be obtained from the Infantry Brigade Headquarters. The Brigade Major was told to collect the operational and training NBC protective equipment for the various parties as ordered.

5.35 p.m. Fire Station Dhaula Kuan

The Fire Fighting Officer had just finished the briefing of his men at the Dhaula Kuan Fire Station. This Fire Station was ordered to take the lead in the disaster mitigation while the other Fire Stations were put on high alert. However, the HAZMAT vehicles along with their crew were ordered to report to the Dhaula Kuan Fire Station at the earliest. The Fire Fighting Officer was worried about their proficiency in handling chemical disasters though they had undergone training imparted by the Army. He decided to check their knowledge and revise any particular aspect in which he felt that they were shaky. He ordered for fifty men with four fire tenders to be ready to move to the site of the disaster within fifteen minutes. He understood the urgency of being at the disaster site at the earliest, but could not endanger the lives of his men. After all, they were trained in fire fighting and not so much in handling chemical disasters. He decided to go with the rescue teams.

5.45 p.m. Fire Station, Dhaula Kuan

The Fire Fighters were ready at the Fire Station with their NBC protective sets. The Fire Fighting Officer asked them to take out the respirators from the sealed packets and put them on their faces. He personally checked the fitting of the respirators and interchanged those that did not fit correctly. He then made them practice the drill of donning the respirator and canister. He ensured that each person was putting on thick full-sleeved shirt and shoes. The overboots would be put on at the site over the shoes. He briefed them once again of the tasks that they were expected to perform and the precautions they should take for their personal safety. By the time he was satisfied it was almost **6.10 p.m.** The team was ready and prepared to take on the task, though the preparations took a much longer time than it takes to take off for a fire accident. They had not forgotten to take the prefabricated showers that they had fabricated and demonstrated to all Fire Stations in Delhi. They could be at the disaster site by **6.40 p.m.**

5.50 p.m. North Extension Market

Almost an hour had passed since Mr. Rajat Chadda had made his first telephone call to the Police Headquarters. He realised that the best contribution he could do to help was to keep himself at this observation post and relay the situation to the police. The situation he could see was not good; in fact it was very serious. He could see people rushing with handkerchiefs on their faces. They were moving erratically without any definite direction. The people emerging from the air-conditioned market below seemed to be more affected. In the market he saw two women in burka moving towards his departmental store. Women in burkas was a very rare sight in this market and they stood out like a sore thumb. It also made Rajat Chadda's thumb twitch; something was not in sync. He telephoned his store manager and asked him to apprehend the persons in burka. He however warned him to take along a few salesmen and be armed with sticks just in case.... He could see his manager and salespersons grabbing the burka-clad persons and dragging them into the shop. Soon the telephone rang and what he heard did not really surprise him. It seemed the two persons in burka were not women but men with breathing contraption fitted on their face; the burka was being used to conceal the breathing masks. They were also carrying satchels containing powder-tin like sealed cylinders. Mr Rajat Chadda wasted no time. He immediately called up Station Commander and the Police Control Headquarters to give a detailed report.

6.00 p.m. North Extension Market

The Police Control Vans had set up roadblocks and diverted the traffic coming onto the North Extension Market area. However, they found it difficult to control the people trying to get away from the area. They couldn't force them since they themselves were in NBC protective gears, but generally convinced most of them to take shelter in a nearby school building, which they had earmarked for medical aid post. They established temporary Control Headquarters and earmarked an office building across the road for establishing the Control Headquarters subsequently. Fortunately, they were in an upwind direction from the market area. They informed the location of the Control Headquarters and Medical Aid Post on radio to the Police Control Room.

6.15 p.m. North Extension Market

The Control Headquarters had got activated. This was the most important portion of the mitigation process. Soon the Police Control Room informed them about the burka-clad terrorists impounded by the staff of the Chadda Departmental Store. They also gave Mr. Chadda's telephone number to the Control Headquarters so that they could maintain direct contact with him. To have a person at such a vantage point where Mr Chadda was situated was always a great relief. The reconnaissance parties of the army and that of the police Rapid Reaction Team arrived and got into immediate action.

6.40 p.m. North Extension Market

The police were relieved as they saw the army column arriving. The balance of the Rapid Reaction Team of the police had also arrived. The officer in-charge contacted the army team commander and together they went to Mr. Rajat Chadda for first hand assessment of the situation. Mr Rajat Chadda was quite clear in his briefing. He suspected that the air-conditioned market had been attacked by the terrorists through the "weather making room" which was on the rear of the air-conditioned market. Besides, the terrorists had been placing powder tin like containers containing chemical agents in litter-bins and other areas where they could not be detected easily. While the medical team proceeded to set the Medical Aid Post, the other personnel moved into the disaster area fully geared with NBC protection gears. The aim of this party was to identify the source(s) of the release of chemical agents and prevent its further spread. They were to identify the agents also, if possible.

6.45 p.m. North Extension Market

The Fire Department personnel had arrived. They sent a team (with chemical agent detectors) along with the army team into the disaster area. One HAZMAT vehicle had also arrived. The Fire Department personnel were quick in selecting a depression in the area for setting up the decontamination point. Simultaneously they sent two fire tenders to the Medical Aid Post so that the casualties could wash their faces and exposed parts of their bodies and decontaminate themselves.

6.50 p.m. North Extension Market

The District Magistrate had reached the disaster site followed by his office staff in separate vehicles. The Station Commander had promised to send the NBC protection gears for them to the Control Headquarters at the disaster site. He had also briefed the Chief Minister on telephone of the arrangements that were being made. He was in constant touch with the army, police, medical authorities, fire department etc. ever since he had received the first telephone call. The Chief Minister had asked him to assess the damage and call him back so that additional help could be sought for. He informed the District Magistrate that he had already appraised the chairman NDMA of the disaster and would seek his assistance in case required. He had also spoken to the Director General Civil Defence and some NGOs to prepare themselves for providing aid. The District Magistrate was aware of the fact that the casualties may be high, and the trauma would be severe. Post-disaster mitigation of psychotic disorder would also require prolonged monitoring. He was happy that the Chief Minister had spoken to the Director General Civil Defence and NGOs for assistance. As he reached the Control Headquarters, the police officer in-charge briefed him of the progress of various parties. The deployment of the army team gave him a lot of mental peace. He started to take over control of the operations. After all it was his responsibility to manage and mitigate the disaster. The greatest job that the "**first responders**", that is, the local public had done, was the quick dissemination of information. Mr. Rajat Chadda's presence of mind deserved recognition.

A Time Map of 20 May 2006

(Can we plan to achieve this target by May 2006)

Time	Events
5.00 PM	• Chemical Disaster at North Extension Market
5.00 to 5.30 PM	• Police Headquarters, Chanakyapuri and Police Control Vans receive message of disaster. • District Magistrate orders reconnaissance party to give situation report. • DIG Delhi Cantonment Area rushes to the site. • Police Control Vans start establishing roadblocks. • OC Field Ambulance and OC Bomb Disposal Company (Army) informed. • Medical Relief Director alerts hospitals.
5.31 to 6.00 PM	• Roadblocks established by Police around disaster area.
6.01 to 6.45 PM	• Control Headquarters established by Police. • The Army and Police Rapid Reaction Teams and Fire Department personnel arrive. • Medical Aid Post and Decontamination Point established.
6 50 PM	• The District Magistrate takes charge.

Fig 1.1 Time Map for Disaster Mitigation at North Extension Market

2

Disaster Management in India

Like the changing seasons, disasters, both natural and man-made, have become recurring events in India and its neighbourhood. India is possibly one of the most disaster-prone countries in the world, due to its climate, geography, geology, vegetation pattern etc. yet very little has been done over the years to prevent or mitigate these disasters. Disasters due to famines, cyclones, floods, droughts, earthquakes, landslides, have become a routine affair. Out of the total states and union territories, more than 25 states are prone to disasters. In addition, the rapid industrialisation has put the country at the risk of a variety of other disasters, which are man-made or technological hazards like transport and industrial accidents, major urban fires and accidents involving hazardous materials etc. While, not all disasters can be predicted and prevented, a state of preparedness and ability to respond quickly to a disaster can considerably mitigate the loss of life, property and human suffering and restore normalcy at the earliest. For example, the phenomenon of earthquakes is sudden, with almost no warning, making it difficult to predict or take precautions. The earthquake map of India has long been prepared dividing it into various earthquake-prone zones of different intensities. The scientists and engineers have also worked out the designs of the buildings to be constructed at these places. However, no importance is given to these guidelines and constructions are carried out regardless, leading to disasters. Strict implementation of quality construction code and adoption of earthquake resistant structures can reduce the impact of earthquakes. As per a United Nations report, "every dollar spent on disaster mitigation saves two or more dollars spent on dealing with or recovering from it."

Mitigation of Disasters

The catastrophic impact of disasters can be considerably mitigated through effective pre-disaster planning and efficient post-disaster management. Some of the essential aspects to be considered for disaster mitigation are:

- A Comprehensive Disaster Management Plan by the District Headquarters for each type of likely disaster in the area of jurisdiction, in consultation with the local medical, police and fire fighting authorities, based on disaster prediction and detailed reconnaissance.
- Prior positioning of emergency resources with existing organisations, at suitable locations based on a well drawn out plan and in keeping with the type of disasters anticipated.
- Impart training to the local population and concerned personnel in the management and mitigation of various types of disasters.
- Rehearsals in the form of simulative exercises to improve upon the efficiency of deployment and training.
- Liaison with concerned authorities for early warning of impending disasters and its dissemination through the media.

- Effective use of the media for guidance of the disaster-stricken people.
- Respond to any such requirement within the country with utmost speed and efficiency.

In disaster management, the cooperation between the people and the government institutions is a very important factor. The organisational structures need to be so designed that the government agencies and volunteer organisations can supplement the efforts of each other. There is therefore a need to create dedicated organisations at the national, state and district levels.

National Disaster Management Plan

In keeping with the federal structure of the country, the responsibility to cope with disasters is essentially that of the State Governments. The role of the Central Government is only supportive in terms of supplementation of physical and financial resources. However, at the national level it is essential that a Disaster Management Plan is evolved so that a holistic approach to disasters in the country can be taken as well as the contingency plans prepared to mitigate the disasters in the states can be monitored. The district administration is the focal point for implementation of all government plans and activities. Therefore, the states and districts should evolve their own plans in a participatory manner, so that state and district specific plans can be formulated.

Disasters can be graded according to their magnitude and capability at various levels to manage and mitigate. For example, at a no disaster situation, surveillance, preparedness, prevention and mitigation activities must be focused on. Some disasters will be within the capabilities of the district whereas others could be beyond the capability of the district but within the capability of the state. However, some disasters may require major direct intervention of the central government at the national level.

Capacity building is critical at all levels. The higher the level of capacity building the lower will be the level at which the disaster can be tackled. Capacity building is a complex long term phenomenon that requires the development of human resources, the establishment of well functioning organisations within a suitable work environment and supportive socio-political environment. Many state governments have Disaster Mitigation and Management Centres such as the Centre for Disaster Mitigation and Management at Chennai and the Disaster Management Institute at Bhopal. At the national level there is a Centre for Disaster Management at New Delhi.

The most important component of preparedness is planning for all contingencies. Resources of different departments have to be harnessed and their working made transparent and accountable by streamlining district, state and national resources and thereby ensuring a smooth lateral and vertical integration to counter any contingency that may arise. Some of the actions that could be taken are:

- Each Ministry, department and organisation at the national level should formulate comprehensive disaster management plans that should dovetail into the national plan.
- Disaster Management plans should be prepared at district level and linked to the state and national plans.
- Standard operating procedures have to be developed and coordinated at all levels, having an "**all hazards**" multifarious approach keeping in view the entire cycle of disaster management for multifarious natural and man-made disasters.

- Infrastructure, maintenance, and safety review should be incorporated in the disaster management plans.
- Implementation and monitoring should be integrated with the planning process.
- **The concept of trigger mechanism** as an emergency quick response mechanism which would spontaneously set the process of mitigation and management into motion should be considered as part of the peremptory process, whereby the receipt of a signal of an impending disaster would simultaneously energise and activate the mechanism for response and mitigation without the loss of critical time.

Legislation and Organisations

With enhanced level of public awareness the field of disaster management has come to acquire a lot of importance in recent times. A suitable legislation with appropriate legal framework at the national and/or state level requires to be provided. There are certain laws relating to various aspects of disaster management which are already existing e.g. coastal regulations, chemical accidents regulations, fire safety regulations etc. However, the implementation and enforcement of these remain weak links in the country.

Weapons of Mass Destruction (WMD) Disasters

Unlike vulnerability to natural disasters, which are generally area specific like earthquakes, floods etc, vulnerability to WMD disasters is not area specific and can be initiated anytime, anywhere. WMD include any weapon or device that is intended, or has the capability, to cause death or serious injury, to a significant number of people through the release of toxic or poisonous chemicals or their precursors, disease organism or radiation or radio activity. Disasters caused due to proliferation and use of nuclear, radiological, chemical and biological agents can be termed as WMD disasters. WMD disasters could take place during war, as the consequence of an accident or it could be perpetrated by terrorists:

- **During War**. Like the dropping of the atom bomb at Hiroshima and Nagasaki during World War II, or chemical attack by the Iraqis on the Kurds during the Iran-Iraq war.
- **By Accident.** The gas leak at the Union Carbide factory at Bhopal or the nuclear accident at Chernobyl are recent examples of such accidents.
- **By Terrorists.** This has been the bane of dual use technology and expertise, which assists the prospects of chemical, biological and radiological terrorism to increase, particularly because of the ease of production and high casualties vis-a-vis low cost. The chemical gas attack in Tokyo sub-way or the September 11 attack at New York are examples of disasters caused by terrorists. Facilities required to produce radiological, biological and chemical weapons are small and difficult to detect, compared to those associated with nuclear weapons. An added dimension is that of the terrorists who kill themselves with the attack and hence require no escape route or plan.

Analysis of various issues related to WMD terrorism clearly indicate our vulnerability to WMD disasters. The probability of vulnerability and consequence could be:

Type	Vulnerability	Consequence
• Chemical and Radiological	Very likely	High
• Biological	Likely	Very high
• Nuclear	Less likely	Very high

The probability of occurrence and the likely impact of various disasters is presented as a pictorial graph in Figure 2.1.

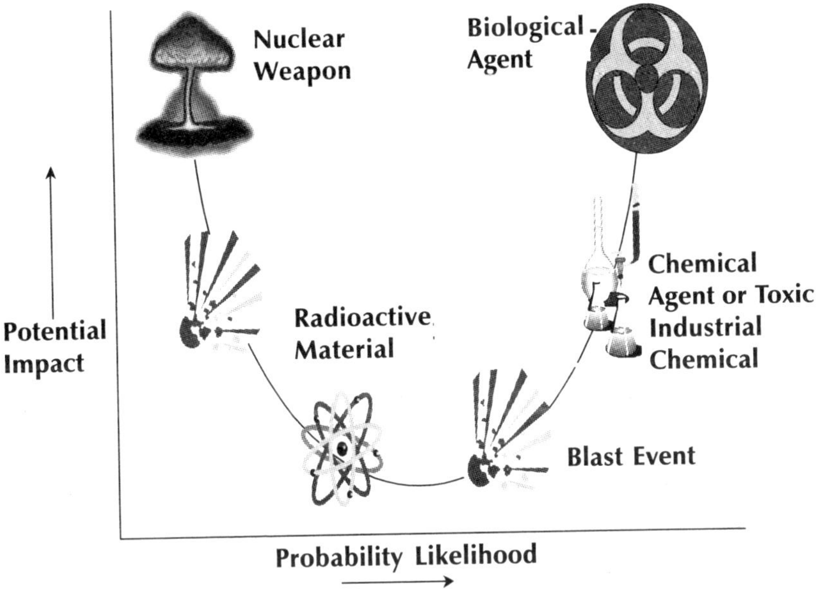

Fig 2.1. Probability-Impact Curve of a WMD Disaster.

It will be seen from the above figure that though the impact of a nuclear strike will be very high, its probability of occurrence is the lowest. On the other hand, the probability of a chemical strike is very high though the impact may be comparatively lower than that of a nuclear strike. Biological strike would account for very high casualties, almost as much as that of nuclear casualties, as well as its probability of occurrence is also very high. The proliferation and ease of availability of chemical and biological agents, sponsorship by a foreign state and the magnitude of the disasters they can cause (for example, a mere 100 gm of Anthrax released over a major city may theoretically cause upto 3 million casualties) warrants that the country be adequately prepared in tackling WMD disasters caused during war, by accident or by terrorists.

Approach to WMD Disaster Management in USA

Countries around the world are applying tremendous resources in many ongoing efforts to improve their Local, State and Federal Governments, WMD response capabilities. In the USA, the Presidential Decision Directive-39 (PDD-39) issued in June 1995 by the White House, entitled "United States policy on Counter Terrorism," recognises that there must be a rapid and decisive capability to protect and provide relief to victims. While many military units possess basic skills and capabilities that can be applied to WMD response requirements, few have been specifically focused on the precise task or equipped with appropriate assets to immediately respond to such an event. Rapid Assessment and Initial Detection Element (RAID) teams of the National Guard of USA have been raised to address WMD disasters. 22 Member National Guard (RAID) teams have been formed in 10 states across the country. Their job is to help civilian authority to detect and assess chemical, biological and nuclear hazards.

The goals during the immediate response phase of an incident are to terminate the terrorist attack, minimise loss of life and property and to provide emergency relief to the affected areas. In responding to terrorist incidents, Federal Department and agencies rapidly deploy the needed federal capabilities to the scene, including specialist elements like RAID for dealing with specific types of incidence resulting from the threat or actual use of WMD. To coordinate the Federal response, the Federal Bureau of Investigation (FBI) and Federal Emergency Management Agency (FEMA) have been assigned lead agency responsibility for crisis and consequence management respectively.

The main features of the American approach to WMD Disaster Management can be summarised as follows:

- A Presidential Decision Directive that recognises the need for a rapid and decisive capability to act against terrorists.
- FBI assigned the lead agency responsibility for Crisis Management.
- FEMA made responsible for Consequence Management.
- Formation of National Guard RAID teams across the country.

Structure and Capability of RAID

The RAID has the capability to rapidly deploy to an incident site and provide initial support to the Incident Commander. The element has the capability to conduct reconnaissance, provide medical advice and assistance, perform detection, assessment and hazard prediction. It also provides technical advice concerning WMD incidents and agents. The RAID has been equipped according to the tasks it has to perform. The organisation of RAID is shown in Figure 2.2.

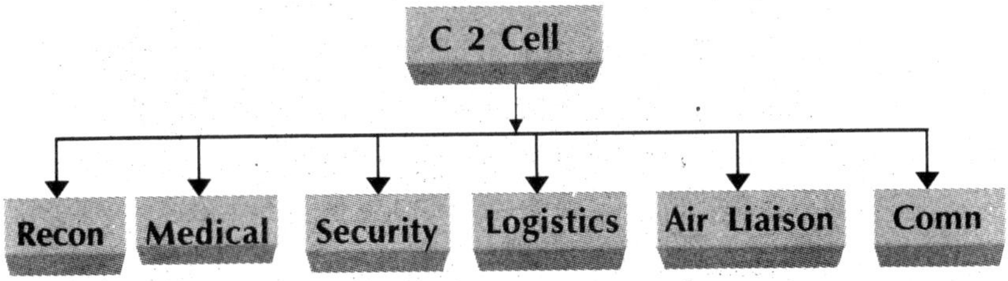

Fig 2.2 Outline Organisation of RAID.

- C 2 Cell provides overall command and control of the assessment team and conducts hazard modelling.
- Reconnaissance Cell provides early detection, initial sample collection and NBC reconnaissance.
- Medical Support Cell provides initial medical assessment.
- Security Cell provides initial assessment of security requirements and manages force protection/assessment element security.
- Logistics Cell determines initial resource requirements and provides supply and maintenance support for the assessment element.
- Air Liaison Cell coordinates the transportation and/or air movement of assessment element.
- Communications Cell provides internal communications within the assessment element, coordinates for communications connectivity with civilian responders, and maintains a reach back capability for additional technical expertise.

Organisations to Mitigate WMD Disasters in India

To respond to disasters including those created by terrorists, India should have an organisation like a National Disaster Management Authority (NDMA). It should be the lead agency to coordinate the consequence management of natural and WMD disasters. Although the affected State and Local Government have primary jurisdiction for emergencies, a terrorist attack involving WMD could create havoc beyond their capability to respond. If this were to happen, that is, if the magnitude of the disaster is high, the NDMA should take over the charge and coordinate the consequence management activities including measures to alleviate damage, loss, hardship and suffering, to protect public health and safety and to restore essential government services to provide emergency assistance. The Intelligence Bureau (IB) could be given the task for Crisis Management response to domestic terrorism which should include measures to identify, acquire, and plan the use of resources needed to anticipate, prevent, resolve a threat or act of terrorism—immediate and post-incident response.

Local response to an emergency situation, should use the Incident Command System to ensure that all responders and their support assets are coordinated for effective and efficient response. The Incident Commander should initially be the senior responder of the organisation with the preponderance responsibility for the event. For example, Fire Chief, Police Chief, Medical Chief, Military etc. and hand over the command to the Civilian Administrator at the earliest instance. If the local assets are inadequate to meet the emergency response requirement, then the State or the National assets have to be requisitioned.

There are some organisations proposed or existing at the national and state level to mitigate natural disasters. Rapid Reaction Teams (RRT), specialised in WMD disaster management should be formed and integrated into these organisations. These should be at the National and State level and be located in the major metropolitan cities, since the vulnerability of large cities is high, considering the disaster and publicity effect that WMD disasters are likely to achieve. These RRTs could be similar to the RAID of the National Guard of USA and should comprise highly trained experts in a cross-discipline of functional areas that can deploy and assess the situation, advise the local, state and national response elements, define requirements, and expedite employment of state and national support. The mission of this organisation should be to provide early assessment, initial detection and neutralisation of the source and also technical advice to the Incident Commander during an incident involving WMD.

Although, the military may have similar organisations, they would be few in number, and more importantly may not be available in times of war. Besides, it is difficult to integrate them permanently with civil organisations since it will affect their primary tasks and responsibilities. Therefore, WMD mitigation teams like RRT should be raised out of organisations like the Central Industrial Security Force (CISF), Indo-Tibetan Border Police (ITBP), Central Reserve Police Force (CRPF) etc. They should be allocated to the states, vulnerable districts, important cities, important infrastructures like the metro railway etc. on a permanent basis, and placed under command the state disaster management organisations for funding, training and maintenance. In addition, at the national level there should be an expanded organisation under command of an organisation like NDMA, which could be the national reserve. It should be possible to offer these teams for out of the country WMD disaster management tasks, when required.

RRT

A recommended organisation for the RRT and the manpower required are shown in Figure 2.3 and Table 2.1.

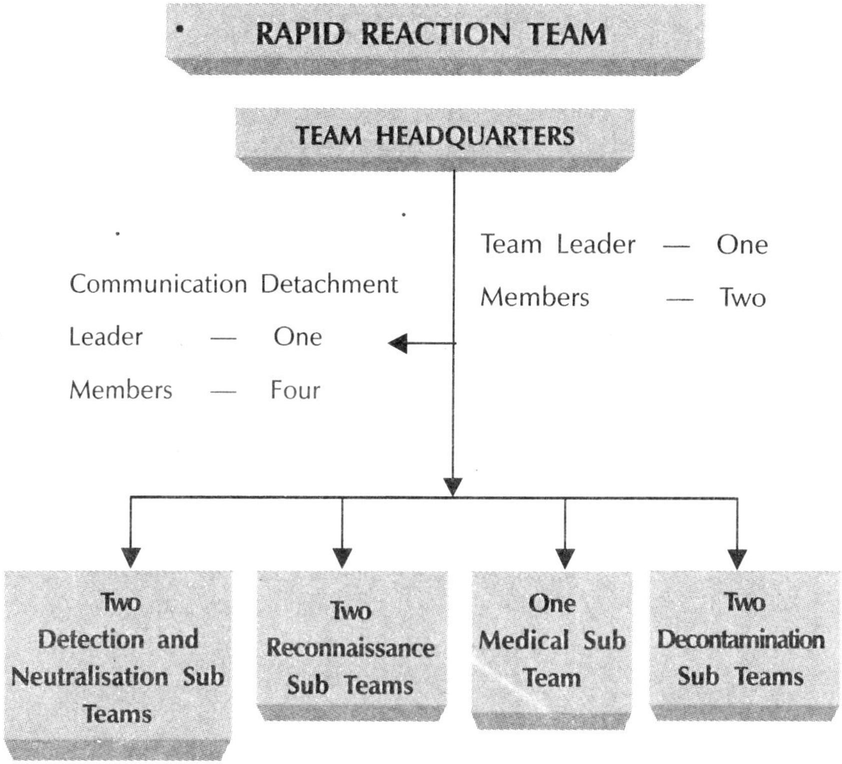

Fig 2.3 Recommended Organisation of RRT

Note: Composition of each Sub Team is one Sub Team Leader and four members.

Type of Organisation	Number of Organisation	Leader	Members	Total
Team Headquarters	One	01	02	03
Communication Detachment	One	01	04	05
Detection and Neutralisation Sub Teams	Two	02	08	10
Reconnaissance Sub Teams	Two	02	08	10
Medical Sub Team	One	01@	04%	05
Decontamination Sub Teams	Two	02	08	10
Total	**Nine**	**09**	**34**	**43**

@ **Doctor**

% **Nursing Assistants**

Table 2.1 Personnel Recommended for RRT

The tasks that can be assigned to the RRT are as follows:

- Assist in the setting up of Control Headquarters.
- Provide reconnaissance teams at short notice.
- Detection of the source of disaster.
- Neutralisation or temporarily plugging the source.
- Monitor the spread of chemical or nuclear contamination.

- Advise higher authorities regarding evacuation of the population to restrict the after-effects of the disaster.
- Provide limited first aid and carry out "triage" of casualties for determining priority for evacuation.
- Assist in making arrangements for quarantining the seriously affected in order to contain the epidemic.
- Assist in decontamination of casualties.

These RRTs should be equipped with "state of the art equipment" being produced indigenously or imported. They should also be provided training in institutions in India and abroad, particularly in the USA and the Czech Republic. Some of the equipment which should be procured for the RRT are as follows:

- Individual protective gears, to include NBC suits, respirators, canisters, gloves and overboots.
- Chemical detection equipment like automatic chemical agent detection and alarm system (ACADA), chemical agent monitor (CAM), individual chemical agent detector (ICAD), three coloured detector paper (TCDP) and residual vapour detector (RVD).
- Radiological detection equipment like personal dosimeter and roentgenometer.
- Decontamination equipment like mobile decontamination system.
- Resuscitators, casualty bags and other medical equipment.
- Drugs and antidotes.

A striking difference in the casualties of WMD disasters vis-a-vis natural disaster is that in case of WMD disasters not only will the number of casualties be high, but also a large percentage of these casualties are likely to be contaminated. The philosophy of dealing with contaminated casualties is in variance with dealing natural disaster casualties. The responders to the disaster will have to be provided protective clothing to prevent themselves from being contaminated. Besides, the medicines required particularly to treat casualties due to chemical agents would be the ones that are not commonly used and hence may not be readily available in adequate quantities. Medical authorities should identify the sources as to where the medicines and antidotes are being manufactured/available off the shelf to enable speedy procurement. In addition, the medical staff will require specialised training in handling the casualties who sustain physical injuries and are contaminated too, as a result of radiological or chemical disasters.

Preparations for WMD Disasters

Preparing for WMD disasters has some inherent problems and difficulties considering the resource constraints as well as the awareness levels of the general public and the various disaster mitigation agencies. Some of them are:

- **Communication of medical authorities**, the public health community, different governmental organisations have interoperable difficulties and lack robust communication systems.
- **Training** carried out mainly focuses on crisis management that terminates in successful resolution of the problem and does not include scenarios where terrorist attacks may be successful requiring consequence management.
- **Mass casualty management** requires overall planning and integration among various agencies. This is lacking at present. It includes medical expertise for all types of WMD and disposition of bodies.

- **Public health surveillance** is lacking and has to be improved to face biological terrorism and emerging infectious diseases.
- **Detection and risk assessment** by first responders and specialised response teams to rapidly and accurately detect, recognise and identify chemical or biological agents and assess the associated health risks may be slow, leading to rapid spread of the hazard.
- **First responders** lack special personal protective equipment to safeguard themselves from chemical or biological agents and could become contaminated themselves.
- **Hospital notification** of the disaster could be delayed leading to contaminated casualties arriving before the hospital has made arrangements to receive and segregate them. They could contaminate other patients and staff unknowingly.

To be prepared for WMD disasters, some of the aspects which require attention in addition to the nuances of natural disasters are:

- Awareness of the general public of the characteristics of various types of WMD disasters, to enable mitigation actions with minimum panic and confusion.
- Provisioning NBC protective equipment and training.
- Provision of detection, alarm and decontamination equipment and training to use the same.
- Training of medical personnel in handling NBC casualties.
- Earmarking dedicated organisations for storing and maintaining the specialised NBC protective equipment and other stores.

- Delegating responsibility to various departments like the Police, Military, Fire Fighting, Medical, Civil Defence, NGOs and last but not the least responsible media.
- Conducting mock exercises with participation from all agencies.
- Training the Civil Administration.

Response to Disasters

Response to disasters can be effective only if plans have been prepared and implemented in the event of a disaster. As has always been experienced, plans are prepared for various contingencies but the disaster that occurs requires a contingency that may not have been fully catered for. The various activities to be undertaken would have to be controlled by organisations with their roles and responsibilities defined unambiguously. Some of the actions recommended to mitigate a disaster effectively are:

- The general public should be aware of the type of disaster and its nuances, so that when warned or informed they can automatically take preventive measures as practised during the preparation period.
- Rapid dissemination of information to all concerned once a disaster is reported. It will help in reducing the time gap between occurrence of a disaster and the response. This dissemination of information should also be done mutually to expedite the passage of information. HAM radio is an excellent unconventional method to disseminate information when other systems breakdown due to the disaster.
- The media must take an active part in warning the people in the vicinity of areas of immediate danger as a result of the disaster.

- Based on the areas affected, evacuation may have to be undertaken to transit locations. The media should be able to guide the people of the exit routes since the police telephone lines will be continuously busy.
- Cordoning off the area by the police and military will reduce the spread of the contamination and should be done at the earliest opportunity.
- In the aftermath of a disaster, search and rescue of victims trapped in contaminated areas will be a problem, thus the provisioning of protective equipment at designated places for the rescue parties is essential.
- A clear and concise post-disaster assessment has to be carried out to identify relief measures and strategies. Based on proper assessment, humanitarian and medical assistance can be sought for as well as utilised effectively. In case of major disasters beyond the capability of the nation to handle, help will have to be sought from international agencies.
- A proper logistic organisation will have to be set up to receive, store and despatch relief materials to disaster victims. It should also have its cells at international airports, the local airport, railway stations etc. so that the assistance is guided to the proper place and handed over to designated personnel. Due to the chaos that is likely to prevail in the aftermath of a major disaster, the relief items may be misappropriated if not handeled properly.
- The primary focus of relief is to provide the basic amenities like medicines, food, water, shelter, health; care to the affected people, to save lives and reduce agony. Distribution of relief material should be based on requirement and not guided by interested parties, as is the common practice.

- Rehabilitation and reconstruction must not be lost focus of once emergency relief operations are over. Victims should be assisted to resume normal lives. Some victims may require humanitarian, psychiatric, medical assistance etc. over a prolonged period of time. The post-disaster phase is as important as the immediate response, if not more.

WMD Disaster Management Information Database

Disasters both natural and man-made cause a lot of damage to life and property. After any disaster, the government, NGOs and various voluntary organisations do focus on the shortcomings that hampered the relief and rescue operations. However, these seldom get incorporated in our drills and procedures due to non-incorporation in an institutionalised database. Initiative on disaster management information database has been taken by organisations like the Society for Research and Initiatives for Sustainable Technologies and Institutions (SRISTI) which was involved in relief and rehabilitation work in Kutch, since they felt handicapped in their operations due to want of information for planning.

Though there is some progress in the creation of a national database, a lot needs to be done in this field. There may be many disaster related databases in the states, but they are not integrated at a national level and hence at the time of disasters much required information is not available readily. A database for WMD disasters should be created at the national level, and kept updated for which a dedicated organisation must be tasked. The environment should be made aware of the existence of such a database, so that they know what is to be done in case of such disasters. In addition, they must be encouraged to contribute authentic information to the database. Towards this end, besides the government organisations specially created to deal with WMD disasters, the civil society, the NGOs and various other voluntary organisations can play a vital role both in creating/updating the databank and in rescue operations. Some of the important issues which merit consideration for inclusion in the database are as follows:

- Warning systems and procedures.
- List of government organisations/NGOs/volunteers to be contacted in case of such disasters.
- Alternate communication networks available.
- Places where various resources, skills and services required during the crises in terms of protective equipment, transport, medicines etc. are available.
- Hospitals earmarked for treating WMD disaster patients.
- List of foreign organisations and agencies specialised in WMD disasters.

Conclusion

Although India has been facing natural calamities and disasters since ages, only knee-jerk actions are taken to mitigate them. For example, the Gujarat earthquake showed our lack of knowledge of the availability of disaster mitigation equipment and their locations and the logistic nightmare of managing the assistance received from all over the country and abroad. The logistics problem in Gujarat was termed as one of "plenty rather than scanty".

The nation has been facing natural disasters, but fortunately has not had to face any WMD disaster so far. WMD disasters are likely to be so sudden that unless adequate preparations are made in advance, mitigation of the disaster and minimisation of casualties will pose a difficult problem. While the organisations for natural disasters mature and stabilise, delay should not be accepted in preparing for WMD disasters, in provisioning equipment for NBC protection, detection and decontamination, training for disaster mitigation, and setting up of organisations like the RRT which may form part of the organisations set up for mitigation of natural disasters.

3

Security Environment and WMD Disasters

The subject of Nuclear, Biological, Chemical Warfare is in itself not new. However, in the recent past it has gained greater importance and these have come to be referred to as the Weapons of Mass Destruction (WMD). India and Pakistan are declared nuclear weapon states and are considered to be fairly advanced in the production and delivery of nuclear weapons. The holding and capability to use chemical weapons is not very transparent. As far as the Biological weapons or the agents are concerned the Biological and Toxin Weapons Convention has no jurisdiction for inspection. Countries continue to carry out research and development of biological and chemical agents for purposes that may often be suspect. This is so, in spite of the fact that they are signatories to the Chemical Weapons Convention as well as the Biological and Toxin Weapons Convention.

Global Trend

The use of chemical weapons by Iraq against the Kurds or as some reports say by Iran against the Kurds during the Iran-Iraq war of the eighties show how ambiguous the knowledge of the use of WMD could be. Whoever was responsible, could this be cited as the major example of the use of WMD since World War II against human beings? The use of chemical agents by the Americans in Vietnam (fortunately not against human beings) signalled the emergence of the use of WMD in warfare. However philosophical one might be, the reality of Nuclear, Radiological, Biological and Chemical Warfare or the WMD has to be reckoned with. For instance, one cannot be certain whether Severe Acute Respiratory Syndrome (SARS) was caused by the leakage or misuse of biological warfare agents.

A number of important political, economic, military and societal trends point towards a world which will continue to be pulled in diverging directions in the foreseeable future. Some current trends are pushing towards globalisation, democratisation, market economies and collective security. Though these trends may be manifest in greater cooperation and interdependence among states, there are major trends pulling towards violence and chaos. These include persistent resource imbalances, propelled by population growth patterns, virulent ethnic hatred and religious fundamentalism. These trends seem to remain as continuing sources of instability and conflict. Nuclear, Chemical and Biological Warfare weapons were till late considered to be assets of countries to be used to deter wars or be used during war. Today, with the worldwide spread of terrorism, the threat of the use of WMD no longer remains during war only, but could be perpetrated during peace also. The one-sided war in Afghanistan and again in Iraq has thrown open all restrictions to terrorism as a result of religious fundamentalism. The unfinished agenda of Palestine and the proxy war waged by Pakistan in India, with Kashmir as the excuse has also opened up frontiers for terrorism to expand in leaps and bounds. Islamic fundamentalism has not spared the Muslim countries either. Saudi Arabia and even Pakistan have been victims of fundamentalist terrorism. Today terrorists have an improved ability to collect information, raise money, and disseminate dogma filled rhetoric. Internet allows the extremists to communicate widely and efficiently and publicly available databases serve as repositories for technical information relating to weapons production. For example, the components required to produce chemical weapons are usually simple products that can be obtained in the free market without any restrictions and a chemical attack can thus be perpetrated using off-the-shelf pesticides sold in grocery stores. The prospects of WMD terrorism and disasters have been enhanced by the changing nature of international terrorism, with its more diversified range of motives, transnational networks, religious fundamentalism and capacity to mount coordinated attacks across the globe.

A major feature of WMD terrorism is its psychological impact which goes many times beyond the physical impact of damage and destruction. The mere thought of exposure to chemical,

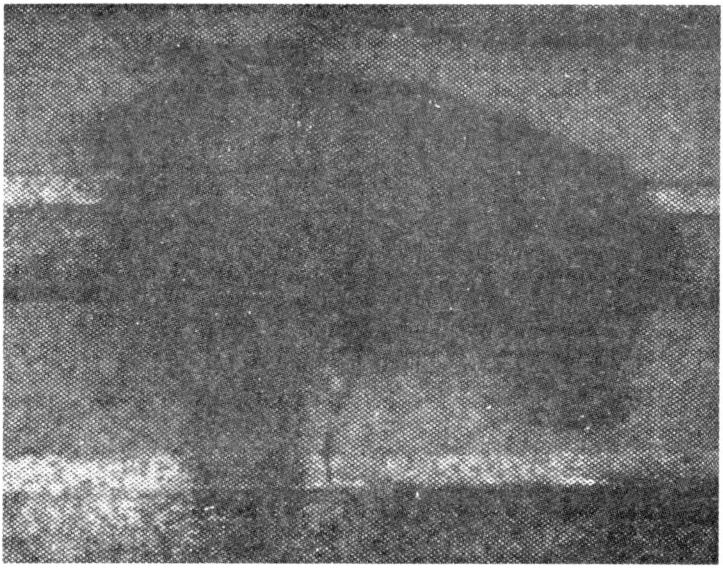

Fig 3.1 Imprint of a Vaporised Man at Hiroshima

biological or nuclear attack takes one's imagination to the pictures of Hiroshima and Nagasaki and causes panic. Figure 3.1 shows the imprint of a man who vaporised in Hiroshima. It is on this platform of psychology of fear that terrorist oganisations germinate their insane philosophy of death and destruction.

The Indian Scene

As one reads the newspaper every day or glues to the electronic media, one realises how our countrymen are vulnerable not only to natural disasters but also to man-made ones. Traffic accidents alone account for approximately one lakh fatal casualties per year. In addition, there are fire accidents in residential areas, accidents due to bursting of gas cylinders, fires due to short-circuiting of electric lines, collapsing of poorly engineered buildings, derailing of trains and the list can be endless. However, most of these accidents can be avoided if laid down rules are followed and the same are monitored religiously by authorised inspection agencies.

As if these tragedies and accidents were not enough, the country is burdened with the activities of terrorists and non-state actors in a continuum from the Punjab militancy in the early eighties to the terrorists in Jammu and Kashmir today. Let us also not forget the ever-increasing state of insurgency and terrorism in our eastern states. The defining feature of non-state actors is action outside the boundaries of established state authority. Their actions could be confined to the territory of a particular state, as in the case of an insurgency, or they could be transnational e.g. terrorists bridging states and even regions. In some cases, non-state actors may enjoy tacit or direct support of countries sympathetic to their goals, and serve as surrogates for states hostile to India. Such state actors have increasing access to WMD that could be seen as providing high payoff for achieving political results from intimidation, disruption and coercion. India has no dearth of terrorists of Indian and foreign origin, foreign agents of Indian origin and agents of foreign origin who have impregnated themselves into the social fabric of India, all of whom remain a cause of concern for the security of India, more so as it relates to terrorists using WMD. The use of WMD by terrorists and non-state actors directly or indirectly supported by state parties is a reality in the context of the "no war no peace" era of proxy war that India is passing through. According to an environmental impact statement of the US Nuclear Regulatory Commission, a large truck bomb used against a nuclear reactor in a highly populated area could cause 1,30,000 deaths. An ordinary conventional explosive could thus be turned into a large radiological weapon. The Tokyo subway type use of chemical agents or spread of diseases through the use of biological agents cannot be wished away. In addition, the low cost proxy war being executed systematically by our adversary in various parts of the country causing fear, panic and deaths is a matter of great concern. Use of WMD in this proxy war may just be a matter of time. Some of the questions that arise are:

- Have terrorists been actively seeking chemical and biological weapons capabilities?
- How easy would it be for terrorists to acquire chemical or biological agents?
- How easy or difficult would it be for terrorists to disperse chemical or biological agents?
- What are the places the terrorists are likely to target for chemical or biological attacks?
- Could terrorists poison the city's water supply?

WMD Terrorism

As dual-use technology and expertise continues to spread internationally, the prospects of chemical, biological and radiological terrorism increase. The relative ease of production of these weapons increases our concern, as far as their availability with terrorists is concerned. WMD terrorism also includes the use or threat to use hazardous materials in an attack on a nuclear/chemical/biological plant for the purpose of causing damage and large-scale casualties. In such cases, the terrorist organisation need not develop, acquire or gain control of a nuclear bomb, chemical or a biological agent in order to cause large-scale damage. It need use only conventional weapons against one of the many nuclear reactors/hazardous industries, seriously damage the same and release hazardous agents.

The proliferation of WMD is widely recognised as the most serious threat to the global security situation. Threats emerging from the proliferation of nuclear, biological and chemical weapons have become one of today's foremost security challenges. This is the result of the increasing availability of the weapons of mass destruction. Official and public attention to proliferation issues, however, has varied over the decades from near hysteric to apathy. In order to understand the present international NBC environment and visualize the future course of events, let us briefly go back into history.

WMD are twentieth-century inventions. From ancient times a military campaign often meant the slaughter of tens of thousands of soldiers and civilians. As the industrial revolution mechanised warfare, the industrialised nations sought ways to kill troops or unprotected populations dispersed over wide areas more efficiently, and to annihilate military and economic targets. Both the Central Powers and the Allies used poison gas for the first time in World War I. Japan used biological warfare in its attacks against the Chinese; at the beginning of World War II. All the belligerent nations had biological weapons research programmes; Germany used poison gas to kill millions of Jews and other prisoners in its concentration camps. At the end of that war, nuclear weapons were used for the first time when the United States struck the Japanese cities of Hiroshima and Nagasaki. Global arsenals peaked during the Cold War decades, when both the NATO nations and the Warsaw Pact countries perfected and produced tens of thousands of chemical, biological and nuclear weapons.

The numbers of these weapons have decreased since, though a greater number of countries now possess WMD. With the Soviet Union and the United States having the majority of the global holdings, they have agreed to reduce their nuclear arsenals and eliminate their chemical and biological weapons. As the threat of global thermonuclear war receded, officials and experts agreed that the propagation of these weapons to others, posed the greatest threat to world security. In January 1992, for example, the member states of the UN Security Council declared that the spread of weapons of mass destruction constituted "threat to international peace and security".

Today, eight nations have nuclear weapons including Israel (which neither acknowledges nor denies their existence). The entire industrialised world, barring a few exceptions like Finland, Austria and Switzerland can be called crypto nuclear powers since they have nuclear weapons stationed on their soil. In addition is the threat of radiological weapons that although not as destructive as nuclear weapons, pose a serious danger, particularly as a terrorist threat. These are weapons that use conventional explosives, such as dynamite, to disperse radioactive materials, including highly radioactive waste material from nuclear power reactors or other non-weapon sources. The international pressure on all nations prohibiting the production of chemical and biological warfare agents may cause non-state parties to develop these covertly.

In the opinion of some authorities, theft of a nuclear device or building a nuclear bomb however crude, are the least possible courses of action for a prospective nuclear terrorist. Far more likely is the dispersal of radiological material to contaminate a target population or area. The material from which "**dirty bomb**" or a radiological bomb is prepared is stored in every nuclear facility worldwide at different levels of security management. There are over 400 nuclear reactors other than special research reactors and nuclear laboratories in the nuclear weapon states. In South Asia alone there are at least seven known research reactors and sixteen nuclear power reactors that not only lend themselves to clandestine procurement of nuclear materials but are also potential targets for terrorist attacks, with consequent release of toxic and radiological materials.

Conclusion

Nuclear weapons may or may not be used by the nuclear weapon states in case of a war and under extreme conditions. Even in the case of Hiroshima and Nagasaki at the end of World War II, it is a commonly held belief that dropping the atom bombs was felt necessary to force Japan to surrender and end World War II. Indeed nothing is farther from truth. To quote Dwight Eisenhower (*Mandate for Change,* 1953-56)

> **"I was one of those who felt that there were a number of reasons to question the wisdom of such an act. I voiced to him (President Truman) my grave misgivings, first on the basis of my belief that Japan was already defeated and that dropping the bomb was completely unnecessary. It was my belief that Japan was, at that very moment, seeking some way to surrender with a minimum loss of face."**

This perception of the use of nuclear weapons may not be true as far as chemical and biological weapons are concerned. Terrorist organisations have been exploring chemical and biological weapons, as is being reported by the media from time to time. Technical hurdles that they may be facing to effectively develop an effective large-scale chemical or biological programme, will be overcome, if not already done. The problem or questions of effectively delivering the toxic chemicals may also arise. The options for delivering these, range from high to low technology as well as innovative means that are innumerable.

While nuclear, chemical and biological weapons are often grouped together as "weapons of mass destruction", each must be considered separately because the effects as well as the disaster mitigation and management requirements will be different. Prior to September 11, 2001, terrorism represented a relatively new concern on the spectrum of disaster management issues. However, domestic preparedness should now become a critical part of the country's overall disaster management planning due to the security environment. Any locality, city or state could be targeted by terrorists from within the country or from outside the country. This is an issue that every leader from the national level to the district level should consider seriously, familiarise with the spectrum of threats and assess the threat to the area of their jurisdiction to ascertain the vulnerable and potential targets.

Terrorists, particularly with the present concept of "jehadis" or suicide attackers, can strike at any place and at any time. Government buildings, monuments, religious places, public venues and even high-profile people can be their targets. There are however, not enough resources to protect every possible target; therefore, preparation to prevent or mitigate disasters should focus on the most likely threat areas, so that budgets and human capital are distributed rationally.

4

Management of Chemical Disasters

Chemical weapons are considered as weapons of mass destruction, since an adversary can use them to cause large-scale destruction of life. Chemical weapons used by the Iraqis against the Kurds during the Iran-Iraq war is one such example in recent times. Thousands died and many are suffering even today from its long-term effects. The high demand for chemicals by industry, agriculture, defence and consumer needs has led to the rapid expansion of the chemicals and petrochemical industries. This has made available various chemicals off the shelf, which when misused could be hazardous. Simultaneously with this expansion the world has witnessed unusually large number of accidents leading to massive releases of hazardous chemicals. The ease with which hazardous chemical agents can be obtained and converted into weapons makes their use by terrorists a high possibility.

To create a chemical disaster it may not be essential to manufacture or activate chemical weapons directly. The terrorists could attack chemical industries where hazardous chemicals are stored and easily create a disaster of unprecedented proportions. Similarly, blowing up of a tanker containing hazardous chemical in a crowded area could also create a chemical disaster.

Chemical Attack During War

India and Pakistan are both signatories to the Chemical Weapon Convention (CWC). Yet the danger of chemical attack during the next war by our adversaries cannot be totally ruled out. It may also result in collateral damage to the civil population due to the close proximity of our villages and towns to our border areas. Ruling out direct chemical attacks against our civilian targets during war may also not be pragmatic. The CWC itself is not foolproof in that it permits member states to conduct chemical defence research, produce chemical defence equipment and continue chemical defence training. The ease with which these apparently defensive actions can change direction to offensive is well understood by the framers of the Convention. To quote General K Sundarji, "Intentions may change overnight, but it takes years to develop capabilities." Therefore, preparation in chemical disaster mitigation, its awareness and training can pay handsome dividends not only during peace time but also during hot war.

Disasters in Chemical Industries

Industrial disasters could be caused by various situations like leak of corrosive material or toxic chemicals from a reaction vessel, storage tank or carrier affecting land and water bodies. The Bhopal gas tragedy in India is a case in point of leakage of toxic chemicals. Disasters could also be caused by explosions involving explosive and inflammable chemicals, or release of highly toxic cloud of gaseous/particulate material spreading by diffusion to neighbouring human settlements. Installations, buildings and private property are the main targets of explosion and fireball formation or leakage of corrosive fluids. Life systems in the vicinity of the site are ready victims in all the situations whether they are "on site" or "off site", or when the released toxic chemicals contaminate the three constituents of the environment, namely, air, water and soil. Dimensions of a chemical disaster are illustrated in Figure 4.1.

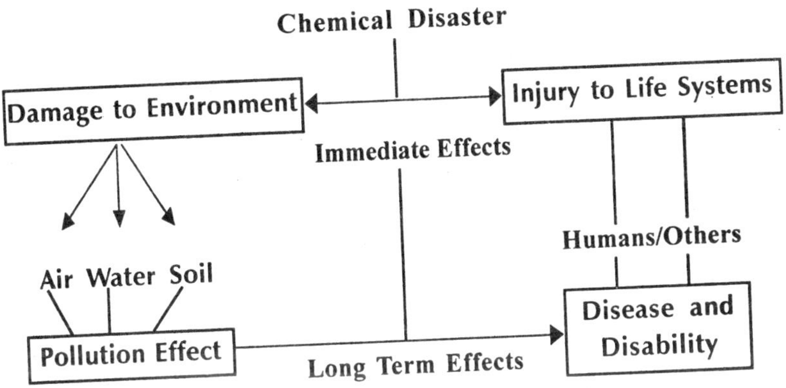

Fig 4.1 Dimensions of a Chemical Disaster

Actions by Industries

It should be mandatory for the industries dealing with potentially hazardous chemicals to chalk out and practise disaster mitigation programmes. Task forces should be formed within the industry itself to ensure that emergency response is available. It may be possible that the emergency response teams of the industry may themselves become victims, therefore, it is essential that such industries should have a tie-up with a similar industry in the near vicinity, on a buddy system, from where the emergency response teams should arrive with the necessary equipment, if required.

In the Bhopal gas tragedy it has been seen that though there were thousands of victims in the area around the industry, there were only a few casualties of night shift workers within the factory itself. This probably goes to show that while the industry takes measures for its protection, it turns a blind eye to the local population around the factory. Through governmental orders it must be ensured that the factory has emergency relief and response teams along with the required equipment to mitigate the disaster outside the factory premises also. If considered appropriate the industry should also conduct awareness programmes as welfare measure, without causing alarm.

Stocks of used hazardous chemicals are also a matter of grave concern. While these chemicals are apparently well protected, possibility of sabotage cannot be ruled out particularly in the present security environment of the country where a 'jehadi' may not be concerned about saving himself while possibly exploding the stocks of chemical wastes. A possible method of securing such wastes that cannot be disposed of is to bury them underground and build structures on it so that the hazard of pilferage or sabotage is totally eliminated.

Disasters Due to Accidents

Hazardous chemicals are often transported from place to place by road or by rail in tankers. Accidents of these load carriers in a city centre or busy railway station could cause very high casualties. Precautions should be taken so that such vehicles do not meet with accidents. Some of the precautions could be to move the vehicles when the traffic is less, the employment of well-experienced drivers and safety personnel, provision of protection and safety equipment in the vehicles, training the crew to mitigate disasters due to accident etc. Depending upon the toxicity of the chemicals it may be worthwhile to send additional security personnel in a separate vehicle or train compartment.

Disasters Due to Sabotage

Sabotage of chemical industries (producing hazardous chemicals or those who have used hazardous chemicals in stock) by terrorists and non-state actors cannot be ruled out. A vehicle containing explosives if detonated in the vicinity of a vehicle containing hazardous chemical will cause a chemical disaster, the magnitude of which will depend upon the type and quantity of hazardous chemical being carried. A possible security measure that could be taken is that the tankers carrying the hazardous chemicals have dummy tankers interspersed so that the terrorists may by default explode the dummy tankers. Another method could be to modify the tankers themselves. The tankers could have a double shell with antidote chemical filled between the two shells to reduce the impact. In the present security environment of the country it may be worthwhile to have armed protection parties in light vehicles along with the convoy of vehicles carrying the hazardous chemicals. Terrorist attacks could be most unpredictable and can take any form and hence it may not be possible to have any full proof system. The only way to prevent them is possibly to have a good intelligence system. The likely targets would be densely populated areas and during periods when the density of people would be high. Therefore, vulnerable areas in the city should be identified and kept under surveillance. A general awareness among the people is also considered advisable without causing unnecessary alarm.

Awareness of Chemical Disasters

It is important that the public are aware of the basic tenets of hazardous chemicals, and likely symptoms in case of an attack. The mitigation measures that should be taken should also be formalised so that the "local response" is effective in case of a disaster. It must be remembered that the local public are the "first responders" in case of a disaster. The greater the awareness and training, the more will be the success in mitigating a disaster, since unlike other disasters, rushing to the spot by rescue teams without appropriate protective equipment is not an answer, instead it may cause casualties in greater numbers. Such awareness should be included in the schedule of training of the Home Guards, NCC cadets etc and they may be made to practise in simulated exercises. They could also hold demonstrations so that the general public is also aware without being unduly alarmed. Another source of creating awareness is through the media, both electronic and print. Posters could also be prepared and displayed in schools, colleges, office buildings and public places.

Characteristics of Chemical Agents

Chemical agents are compounds which when suitably disseminated produce incapacitating, lethal or damaging results leading to chemical disasters. The disseminated chemical could be in the form of:

- Liquid droplets or spray, like rain.
- Liquid aerosols, like fine mist, small enough to be inhaled.
- Solid aerosol, like smoke.
- Vapour or gas.

It is important to know about the chemical agents so that defensive measures can be adopted once affected by such agents. For the persons severely affected this knowledge may not be of much use; however, the persons who are some distance away from the place of discharge or who have not been severely affected may be able to take protective measures to help themselves from fatality. For example, wetting a handkerchief with water and placing it on the face will protect a person for some time from chemical agents.

The duration of effectiveness, that is the time for which the agent remains effective will depend on factors, like physical characteristics of the agent, the amount of agent present and its physical state, the manner in which the chemical agent has made its presence, the weather in the area where the chemical has been dispersed and the nature of the area itself or terrain. From the point of duration of effectiveness the chemical agents may be classified as "persistent and non-persistent agents".

- **Persistent agents** continue to present a hazard over the area for a considerable period after delivery. These are normally delivered in liquid droplet form, either through munitions or by spraying and are comparatively less volatile. The chemical hazard may be in the form of contact of the liquid or by production of chemical vapour over a prolonged period.
- **Non-persistent agents** disperse rapidly after release and present an immediate short duration hazard. They are volatile and primarily attack through the respiratory route.

Chemical agents may be disseminated in vapour form so as to be inhaled (respiratory attack) or delivered in the form of a liquid to be absorbed through the skin (percutaneous attack). There is no definite boundary between the two, therefore, a respiratory attack may have some secondary percutaneous effects and vice versa. In fact, a combined threat with greater respiratory attack and a secondary percutaneous attack would be more common.

The chemical agents can be categorised according to the physiological or psychological action on the human body. The important ones are:

- Nerve agents.
- Blister agents

- Blood agents.
- Choking agents.

Nerve agent is the most toxic and dangerous of the lethal chemical agents. Major method of their entry into the human body is through the respiratory route. However, the vapour is readily absorbed by the eyes and by the tissues in the nose and throat. When dispersed as vapour, spray or aerosol, they are also absorbed through the skin. Most nerve agents are quick acting particularly when inhaled, with some symptoms developing within one to two minutes after inhalation. They act comparatively slowly when penetration is by absorption through undamaged skin. Liquid nerve agents penetrate ordinary clothing rapidly. However, significant absorption through skin requires a few minutes, and therefore contaminated clothing can be removed and the agent washed off. Nerve agents on the skin can be easily removed by using Fuller's earth (*Multani Mitti*) or by washing with soap and water. The casualties caused by nerve agents may range from mild disability to death depending on the dose received and the adequacy and speed of counter measures taken and medical aid rendered.

Nerve agents cannot normally be detected by human senses. Hence, it is necessary to use vapour and liquid detection instruments to detect and monitor chemical agents. Some of the instruments are Automatic Chemical Agent Detection and Alarm System (ACADA), Chemical Agent Monitor (CAM), Residual Vapour Detector (RVD), Three Coloured Detector Paper (TCDP) etc.

Persistent nerve agents are practically colourless and relatively less volatile liquids, which slowly emit an odourless toxic vapour. Their consistency is the same as that of light lubricating oil and their persistency is such as to make them extremely hazardous as a liquid or as an aerosol which could be inhaled, absorbed through the skin or swallowed with contaminated food or water.

Non-persistent nerve agents are also practically colourless and odourless and are highly volatile. They vaporise rapidly into a highly toxic cloud. Their consistency is similar to that of petrol. They normally present a vapour hazard that attacks through the eyes and respiratory tract, but may also penetrate normal clothing to attack through the skin.

The order of the onset of symptoms of nerve agent poisoning varies with the type of chemical agent. The characteristic signs and symptoms of a nerve agent attack are:

- Blurring of vision and pinpointing of pupils.
- Severe frontal headache, excessive sweating and watering of nose and eyes.
- Tightness of the chest with difficulty in respiration and wheezing sound due to constriction of bronchia.
- Vomiting, diarrhoea and severe pain in the abdomen.
- Muscular twitching and fasciculation and in-coordination of muscles.
- Apprehension, giddiness, emotional instability, slurred speech and cyanosis.

Saving of life depends on early recognition of nerve agent poisoning. They can be identified by characteristic signs and symptoms, on the basis of the time interval between positioning and appearance of symptoms. These can be divided into the following categories:

- **Early**. Running nose, increased salivation, tightness in the chest, dimmed vision and difficulty in breathing. One must recognize these symptoms, move away from the area, wash oneself and seek medical assistance.

- **Late.** Headache, drooling and excessive sweating. At this stage also first aid and self-aid can save a casualty.
- **Dangerous**. Involuntary urination and defecation, twitching and jerking of muscles. Hope of saving a casualty at this stage recedes.

The essential elements of management of nerve agent poisoning are termination of exposure, decontamination, assisted ventilation with respirators and injection of atropine and oximes e.g. pralidoxime chloride, obidoxime etc (this requires medical assistance). It must, however, be remembered that in case the casualty is not affected by a nerve agent, administering of atropine is harmful and may cause atropine poisoning. Another medicine that has shown to be useful in the therapy of nerve agent poisoning is diazapam that possibly acts by virtue of its anti-convulsive properties.

Blister agents affect the eyes and lungs and blister the skin. Hot and humid conditions and sweat-prone parts of the body are more conducive to attack. The principal blister agent is a persistent liquid known as mustard, which gives off a vapour with slight but characteristic odour of garlic. They may appear as colourless to dark brown, oil liquid droplets, but are normally invisible in vapour form. In liquid or vapour form, these agents may burn or blister any part of the body that they contact, either internally or externally. Blister agents, which come in direct contact with the eyes, may produce marked effects such as redness, inflammation and frequently temporary blindness. Inhalation of blister agents may cause serious damage to tissues in the mouth, nose, throat and lungs.

Liquid mustard penetrates normal clothing in a few minutes, vapour takes considerably longer. Severe internal injuries will also result from the consumption of contaminated food and drink. Mustard in low concentration is normally not lethal, but it is a high casualty product and heavy doses cause permanent injury, sometimes fatal. The degree of damage depends upon the type and concentration of the agent, the weather, the degree of activity of the individual and the exposure time.

Mustard acts insidiously on the eyes; it penetrates without causing pain and after a few hours manifests as lacrimation and a sensation of grit in the eyes; the conjunctiva and the eyelids become red and swollen, blistering of eyelids may also take place alongwith conjunctivitis and corneal lesions. In mild conjunctivitis, recovery takes place in 1-2 weeks, while in severe cases recovery may take place in 2-6 weeks. The risk of leaving liquid vesicant in the eyes is much greater than the risk from exposure of the eyes to vesicant vapours during short period of decontamination. Moreover, the speed of decontamination is very vital since it has little value if carried out after more than two minutes.

An outstanding characteristic of the action of mustard is its insidiousness. If only a small dose is applied to the skin there is itching and burning and the effect is limited to erythema (redness and swelling). Erythema gradually disappears and the colour changes from red to brown resembling sunburn. Except with mild vapour burns, erythema is followed by vesication (formation of fluid). With higher dose, blister formation starts generally between 12 to 48 hours after contact. The blister usually ruptures spontaneously giving rise to open wounds. At times differentiation between mustard lesions and those produced by arsenicals may be difficult.

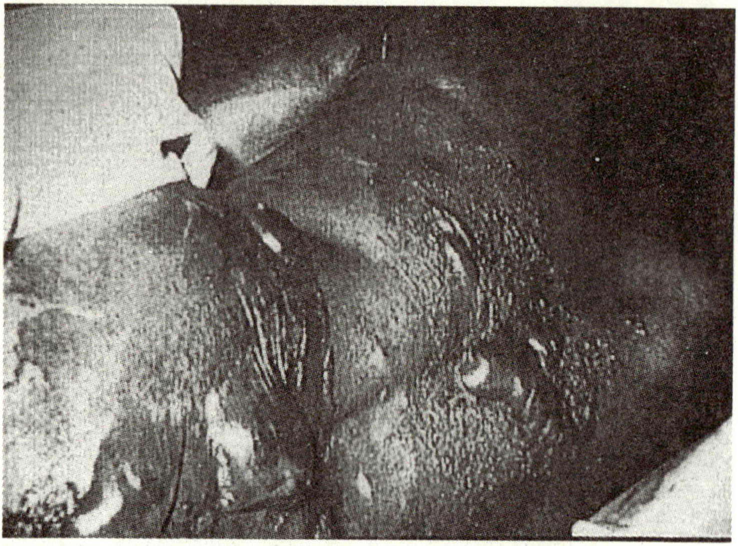

Fig 4.2 Effect of Blister Agent

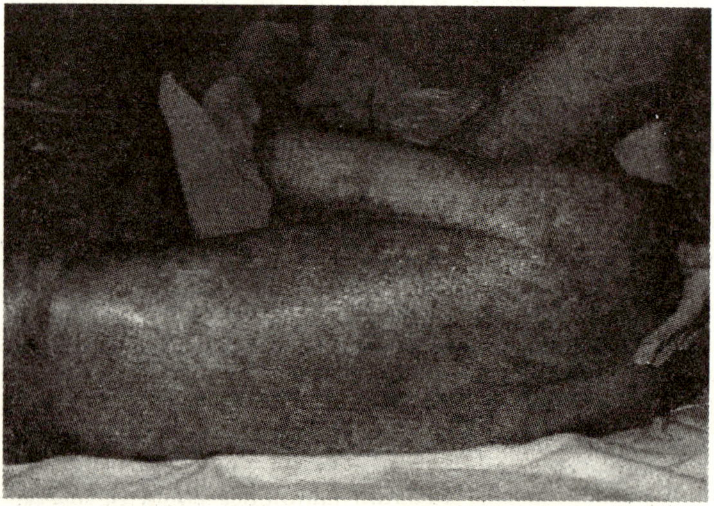

Fig 4.3 Effect of Mustard Agent on Skin

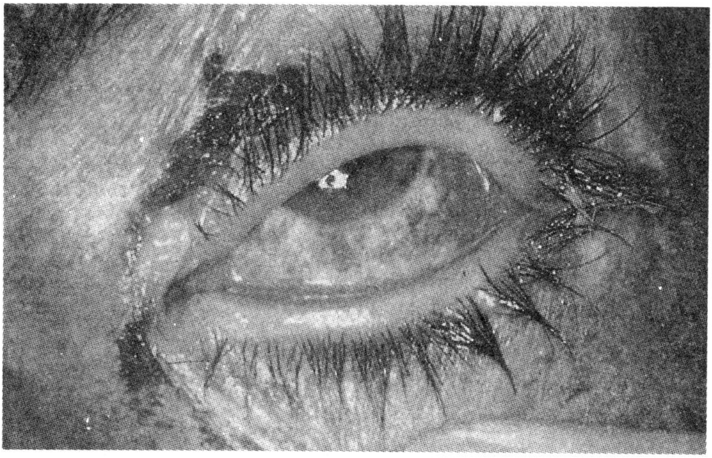

Fig 4.4 Effect of Mustard Agent on Eyes.

Mustard vapour also damages the respiratory tract, and the lesions develop after 4-6 hours. The symptoms are nasal secretion, burning pain in the throat; the voice becomes hoarse after vocal chords become paralysed, breathing becomes difficult, and injury to the lung tissue causes secondary infection leading to bronchopneumonia. If mustard is ingested it leads to destruction of mucous membranes. The symptoms are nausea, vomiting, pain, blood diarrhoea, prostration and shock.

Self-aid in case of mustard attack is to leave the area affected at the earliest and wash the eyes preferably with normal saline on clean water. Clothing should be removed and the skin decontaminated with Fuller's earth. Medical aid would include putting towels soaked in two per cent aqueous solution of chloroamine-T. Bland calamine lotion can be used for minor blistering; pain can be relieved by using analgesics; cough can be relieved with patent cough mixture, steam inhalation and broad spectrum antibiotics could be used in moderate and severe cases. It is better to leave the mild respiratory tract injury cases to the nature to heal.

Blood agents are colourless, have an odour of bitter almonds and are usually disseminated as vapours or gases and are absorbed by inhalation. In liquid form, they can be absorbed by the skin. In both forms, blood agents are non-persistent as their boiling point is low. Blood agents prevent the utilization of oxygen carried by the blood at the cellular level, thus causing the cells to die. Hydrocyamic acid and cyanogen chloride are important blood agents. Inhaling hydrogen cynamide may produce symptoms within seconds and death within minutes. Acute poisoning is characterized by dizziness, headache, palpitation, anxiety, dyspnoea, convulsions, paralysis, coma, cardiovascular collapse, respiratory arrest etc. With the onset of symptoms like pink colour of skin, increased depth of respiration, convulsions etc. prompt medical assistance is required failing which a person may die within few minutes.

Choking agents are colourless with a suffocating odour reminiscent of mouldy hay. They are usually disseminated as gases. The best known of these is phosgene which is a non-persistent chemical agent. Phosgene accounted for some 85 per cent of all deaths attributable to chemical weapons during the First World War. These agents are taken into the body by inhalation. Unlike other agents it has no effect on the skin. They affect the respiratory system by damaging the lungs and, in extreme cases, causing them to fill with fluid.

During or immediately after exposure to dangerous concentration of phosgene the following signs and symptoms develop:

- Irritation of the eyes, throat and respiratory tract with lacrimation, coughing and choking.

- Feeling of tightness in the chest, nausea and vomiting.
- After a latent period of 30 minutes to 24 hours there may be more significant symptoms and signs that may be precipitated with exercise.
- Increasing quantities of frothy white or yellowish fluid may be expectorated. Later the fluid may become pink tinged.
- Circulatory collapse and cardiac failure may occur.
- Almost eight per cent of fatal cases succumb within the first 48 hours of exposure.
- Often the symptoms may be followed by a latent period of two to four hours during which the individual appears to have recovered. The delayed effects include rapid and shallow breathing, painful cough, discomfort and fatigue, shock and frequently death.

As self-aid/first aid the casualty should be removed from the area immediately. Decontamination is not necessary. The casualties should be made to rest and provided warmth.

Incapacitating agents are non-lethal psychochemicals which produce physical or mental effects of sufficient severity to prevent humans from carrying out their normal tasks. Riot control agents like CS agent or mental incapacitating agent like BZ fall in this category. These agents can produce temporary paralysis, persistent lachrymation, diarrhoea, vomiting, convulsive spells of mental confusion etc. Table 4.1 lists some important chemical agents and their symptoms and treatment are given in Appendix 'A'.

Types of Chemical Agents

Sl. no.	TYPE	NAME
1.	Nerve Agent	Tabun (GA) Sarin (GB) Soman (GD) VX
2.	Blister Agent	Distilled Mustard (HD) Nitrogen Mustard (HN1 to HN3) Lewisite (L)
3.	Blood Agent	Hydrogen Cynide (AC) Cynogen Chloride (CK) Arsine (SA)
4.	Choking Agent	Phosgene (CG) Diphisgene (DP) Chloropicrin (PS)

Table 4.1 Names of Some Chemical Agents.

Process of Mitigation of a Chemical Disaster

A chemical disaster scene may or may not be indicative immediately on occurrence. Vapours from chemical agents may be colourless, odourless and therefore it will be difficult to identify the source of the deadly agent. It will only come to notice if there is a discriminating odour, or people around are developing symptoms due to the effect of the chemicals. By the time people in the vicinity realise that there is a chemical attack or leakage of a chemical source large number of persons would have been affected. There is therefore a likelihood of time delay from the time the chemical hazard is activated, to the time when the same is reported. Panic would set in and in crowded areas, a stampede may result in people trying to exit as rapidly as possible from the area. During this period the contaminated persons will be moving in different directions to escape, thereby spreading the effect of the chemical to greater distances. In case the chemical is a liquid persistent agent it is then likely to be carried by the contaminated persons, in whichever direction they move. The speed of the wind and the ambient temperature will also assist in the dispersion of the effect of the chemicals. If the chemical is only in gaseous form, then the persons will be more affected through oro-nasal route and less through skin. Their clothes however will be contaminated, though to a lesser degree. While reporting to the police therefore, it should be intimated whether the chemical is in gaseous form or liquid spray form. At this stage it will be difficult to control the panic. However, if there is adequate awareness of chemical disasters among the general public, then the "first responders" should form out of the local people. The first responders should direct the people to move away from the site of disaster and in a direction opposite to the direction of the wind prevailing, as shown in Figure 4.5.

However, they would not have any sense of direction and may possibly take the path that the discharged gas is taking or the direction that is being swept by the wind. Depending upon the type of gas, people would be dead, or writhing in discomfort due to the choking of the oro-nasal tracts, or struggling to get out of the area if comparatively less affected. The types and numbers of casualties caused would vary with the type of chemical agents. It would also depend upon the environmental conditions like temperature, wind velocity, humidity etc.

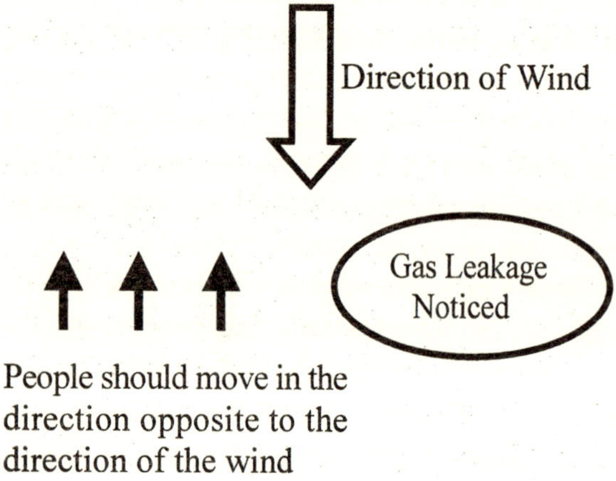

Fig 4.5 Direction of Movement of People.

Reporting the Disaster

In case of any disastrous event or accident the tendency is to telephone the police because the police is considered to be the custodian of a civilized society. In every town or city there should be a telephone number known to the common people, through which they can contact the local police. For example, the people of New Delhi are familiar with the telephone number "100" for Police. But will the police react if they receive a message or information of a gas/chemical disaster? They will probably advise the caller to call the Fire Station. The Fire Station in turn may not react since it is not a case of fire. The most important contribution of the police would be to inform the various departments responsible for disaster management like the civil administration, the armed forces, medical services, fire department etc. The police should also activate the mobile police vans and inform other police stations. However, the police would take these actions only if they are tasked to do so.

First Responders

The first responders of any chemical disaster are the affected local population. It is essential therefore that through regular awareness training and simulated exercises, the people should be educated on the actions to be taken in case there is a chemical disaster. The media, particularly television and the radio should help in the capacity building of awareness among the common man. However, it should be done in such a manner that it does not cause alarm. For example, there should be periodic announcements and television broadcasts that in case any leakage of gas is detected anywhere, the local police should be immediately informed indicating the place of the accident and the general apparent symptoms. In addition, basic symptoms of some agents could be communicated periodically on television.

The Police Force

The police can only react to chemical disasters if they are trained, equipped and tasked. The police should be tasked to respond to any WMD disaster and Standing Operating Procedures (SOP) should exist in the police stations listing out the actions to be taken. If it requires any legislation to enhance the Charter of Duties of the police, then the same must be done. It should be clear to the police that WMD disasters like any other accidents are also their responsibility and their limits of responsibility should be unambiguously defined. The police may require to project additional requirements in terms of men and materials to handle this task. The responsibility of the police and a sequence of action that they could adopt has been discussed later in the chapter. There could be many variations to the sequence of action suggested depending upon the preparedness of the force, the location of the disaster, the magnitude of the disaster and the type of disaster and the chemicals involved. In any case, the police force would be the first to reach the scene or outskirts of the disaster area. Their speed of reaction and efficacy would depend upon the training and equipping to face such disasters. The police would therefore become the second responders to the disaster.

On receiving the telephone call intimating the disaster, the police should intimate its static and mobile patrols in the city, so that, those detailed, home on to the site of the accident immediately. Simultaneously, they should inform their higher headquarters to inform at the appropriate level all concerned like the local military headquarters, civil defence, medical authorities, fire department etc. The police have the best communication networking in a town or city. Informing all concerned of the disaster should, therefore, primarily be the responsibility of the police.

For the police to be effective in an area of chemical disaster it is essential that they are adequately protected for the task. It is recommended that each police station should have some individual protection equipment. Approximately one hundred sets of NBC individual protective equipment should be available in a specified police station of the district. These should be maintained in hermetically sealed packing as they are received from the manufacturers and converted to training stores once the life expiry period is over, and simultaneously replaced. The "police control vans" must at all times carry a few sets of NBC gear depending upon the number of persons generally travelling in these vehicles. A list of items recommended for protection of personnel is given in Table 4.2. All these items are manufactured indigenously and are available ex-trade (on order). Rough cost of these items and the vendors manufacturing the same are given in Appendix 'B'. It would be ideal if the police could also be provided with NBC suits. However, this being an expensive item and not yet indigenously manufactured, it could be procured once structures for WMD disaster management take concrete form.

Sl. no.	Item	Qty	Approx Cost
1.	Respirator	1	Rs 1900
2.	Canister (life 2 hours)	3	Rs 404
3.	Personal decontamination kit	1	Rs 125
4.	Rubber gloves (outer)	1pair	Rs 350
5.	Cotton gloves (inner)	1pair	
6.	Overboot	1pair	Rs 800
7.	Haversack (to keep the items)	1	Rs 500

Table 4.2 List of Protective Equipment for Individuals

With the tasks and commitments that the police have, it may not be possible to train all the personnel in NBC warfare. However, a percentage of officers should be sent to take NBC courses, while the remainder should be given awareness training and training to don the protective equipment. Periodically short cadres could be conducted, so that capacity building for awareness can progress without adversely affecting their primary duties.

Police training should also include information circulation to the concerned people, directing police forces nearby to the site of the disaster, setting up of adhoc Command and Control headquarters with essential communications, providing a firm base for other oganisations to establish themselves depending upon their tasks and responsibilities.

Cordoning off the Area

In a natural disaster, quicker the relief appears on the scene of the accident, the greater are the chances of saving lives. In the case of a chemical disaster the faster the area is cordoned off, the lesser will be the casualties due to the disaster. No person should be allowed to enter the disaster area nor should anyone be permitted to leave the area (as far as possible). This is easier said than done, because the rush both to and from the area of disaster is likely to be very high and it may be difficult for the police to place an absolutely tight cordon as would be appropriate. The cordon may have to be established in two circles. The inner circle could be as close as possible to the area of disaster and an outer cordon a few kilometres away to stop people who are not aware of the disaster, visitors and sight-seers from going to the site of disaster. This will also ensure that the incoming routes are not cluttered with traffic, which would slow down or prevent assistance in the form of water tankers, ambulances, medicine carrying vehicles etc. from reaching the site of disaster. The two circles of cordon are shown in Figure 4.6.

Control Headquarters

When there is chaos of any nature, people look forward to discipline to bring the chaos to control. Setting up of an adhoc Command and Control structure is therefore an immediate requirement. No body of people is more in demand than people in uniform when in chaos. The police which is in the process of setting up the cordon is the ideal force to set-up a Control Headquarters. The Control Headquarters should be set up near a police check-post in a direction opposite to the direction of the wind. The location of the Control Headquarters should be intimated to all concerned so that people providing assistance report to the Control Headquarters. A covered area or building should be selected close to the Control Headquarters to be designated as an emergency Medical Aid Post.

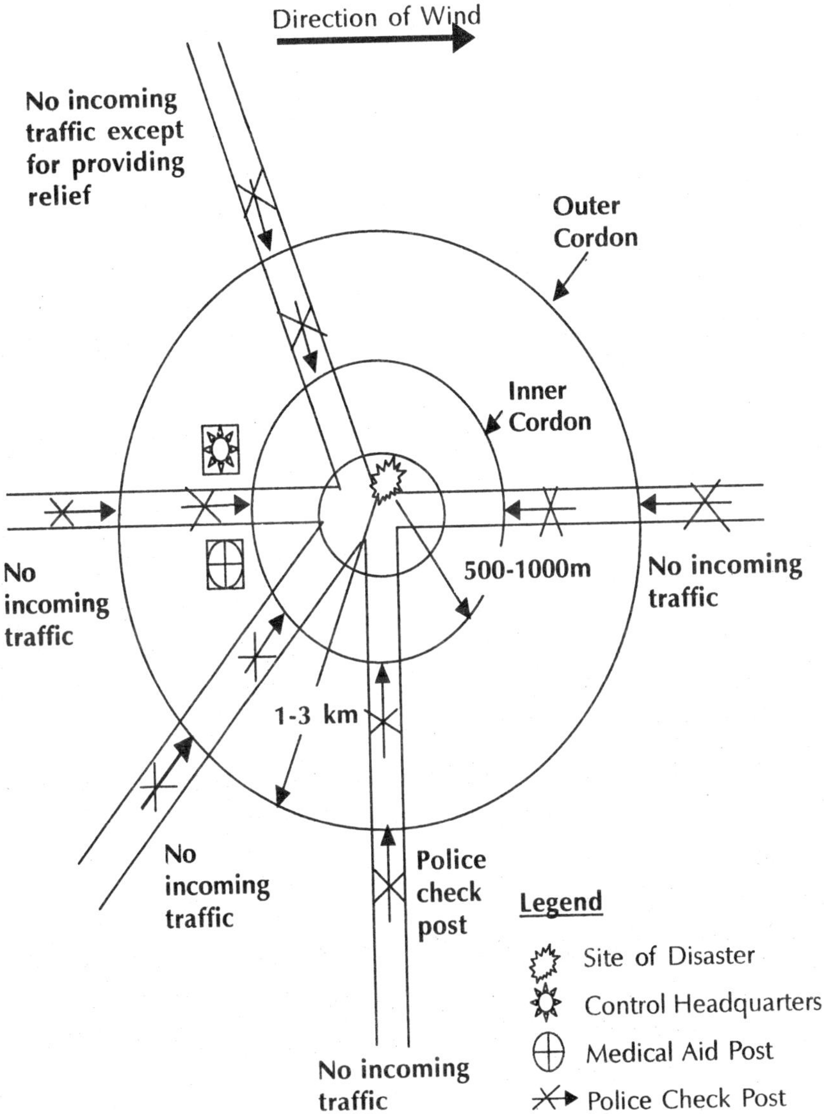

Not to Scale

Fig 4.6 Cordoning off the Chemical Disaster Area by the Police

The Armed Forces

The response of the military, particularly the army, will depend upon the proximity of the army units to the area of disaster. Some cities and towns have military Station Headquarters while others do not have and are dependent on the military units of cantonments in the near proximity. Civil-military liaison at state / district /city level for all purposes is an effective on-going process. For example, Delhi Area Headquarters located at Delhi Cantonment is responsible for all civil military actions in and around Delhi. The Andhra Pradesh, Tamilnadu and Karnataka Area Headquarters (AT &K Area) located at Chennai is responsible for the states of Andhra Pradesh, Tamilnadu and Karnataka. Under the Area Headquarters there are many Sub-Area Headquarters responsible for various areas. For example, Bangalore Sub-Area located at Bangalore is responsible for Bangalore city and nearby areas. It is important therefore, that in the periodic civil military liaison conferences, management of WMD disasters should be a mandatory agenda item. In addition, there are various Air Force and Naval Stations which will provide necessary help when required. It is essential that each of these headquarters have adequate number of sets of individual protective equipment as given in Table 4.2. It is recommended that about 200 sets should be available in the vicinity of the headquarters for quick deployment of the troops. In addition, the army contingents should be accompanied by water tankers (as many as possible) and should home on to the Control Headquarters set up by the local police. Depending upon the magnitude and additional troops required, additional protective equipment could be moved in from nearby military units. The following tasks are envisaged to be carried out by the armed forces:

- Evacuation of casualties to the Medical Aid Post.
- Manning of control points at the periphery of the exclusion zone, along with civil police, to prevent entry/ exit into the contaminated area.
- Aiding in decontamination of personnel.
- Helping the civil and medical authorities to evacuate casualties to hospitals.
- Assisting the police in maintaining law and order.

Armed Forces Teams including Medical Personnel

The armed forces have well-trained and equipped teams including medical personnel. They should ideally be deployed to detect the source and type of chemical and try and seal the source of the leakage/disaster. This will prevent the spread of contamination as well as assist the medicos to be certain of the treatment required. The personnel from the fire department should work in close liaison with these personnel of the armed forces. Since these teams are likely to be available only in certain major cities, arrangements have to be made to move the nearest team by the fastest means to the location of the disaster so that they are effective at the earliest. Some of the teams from other cities should also be moved to the site of the disaster by the fastest means in case required. The armed forces headquarters will be responsible for directing the units to the site of the disaster. The local Military Station Headquarters should have standing operating procedures prepared, so that they issue the necessary request for mobilising the teams locally and across the country. These teams should report to the Police Control Headquarters established at the site of disaster. They could be tasked to undertake the following:

- Rescue mission by fully equipped and trained troops.
- Detection, identification and monitoring of the chemical agents.
- Decontamination to sanitise contaminated personnel.
- Provide first aid to the casualties.
- To assist in the evacuation of casualties out of the contaminated area to the medical aid post.
- Provide specific treatment to casualties.
- Assist in evacuation of casualties to earmarked hospitals.

The Fire Department

What would the fire department do where there is no fire? Well the fire service people are the only people who are actually trained to manage hazards, and are also equipped to a great extent depending upon the city where they are located. For example, the fire department of New Delhi has the rupees four crores worth "Hazmat vehicles" with chemical and nuclear detection and decontamination equipment as well as equipment required for other hazards for disaster management. It however does not have detection equipment for chemical agents like nerve agents, blister agents, blood agents etc. The fire department personnel should have individual protective equipment at the respective fire stations. Detection of the source and type of chemical is a very important activity. The fire stations should also have with them equipment like portable gas chromatograph, chemical agent monitor and chemical agent detector and alarm system. Since the personnel deployed for detecting the source of the disaster will have to approach the site of the disaster, it is recommended that they be provided with NBC suits.

An additional important task by the fire department would be to set up decontamination points. To operate the decontamination set up, it is imperative that they are provided with decontamination suits. Since the number of firemen operating in the decontamination points may not be adequate, it is recommended that fire stations are equipped with additional decontamination suits to be given to personnel who assist them in decontamination. In setting up the decontamination centres, the water tankers and hosepipes of the fire department will be very useful. The department should also be provided with wherewithal to set up light prefabricated shower points with plastic sheet covers. Method of setting up decontamination centres has been discussed later in the book.

Medical Assistance

On receiving intimation from the medical authorities and the control centres, the hospitals in the near vicinity must gear up immediately to accept the casualties. Isolation wards must be vacated, reception and decontamination centres should be created, and medical teams (less the medical personnel to be dispatched to the site of disaster) formed. Depending upon the magnitude of the disaster hospitals in adjacent cities and towns must also be warned and prepared to accept the casualties. Modifications required and procedure to be followed on receiving the casualties is discussed in detail in Chapter 8. Each and every hospital should have their own well-practised WMD Disaster Management Plans.

Each and every hospital in the country should have trained medical staff who could form small medical teams and operate independently in case of a chemical disaster. These medical teams will be required to operate in the area of disaster and should therefore have individual protective equipment. Depending upon the number of medical teams and the number of persons in each medical team the hospital should be adequately equipped with protective equipment and standard medicines and drugs. Nominated hospitals in cities and districts should have casualty evacuation bags to be sent with the medical teams to the disaster area. A suggested composition of the medical team is as follows:

- Medical Specialist - 1
- Anesthetist (if available) - 1
- Medical Officer - 1
- Operating Room Assistant - 2
- Nursing Staff - 6

On receiving intimation from police through the medical department of the town or city, the medical teams would rush to the site of the disaster and report to the Control Headquarters set up by the police. For speedy passage of information, it is important that the police control room knows the contact number and addresses of the medical authorities who will mobilize the medical teams of the hospitals, as also provide advance warning to the hospitals to be ready to accept chemically affected casualties. Once the teams of the armed forces and fire department have been able to identify the type of chemical, the on-site police control room will report the same to the medical authorities. In any case, they will intimate the symptoms of the persons affected, so that the medical teams arrive adequately prepared with the immediately available requisite drugs, and the remaining medicines could follow. The report to be sent to the medical authorities should include the following:

- Place of disaster.
- Nature of disaster.
- Symptoms exhibited by the casualties.
- Location of the Control Headquarters.
- Approximate number of casualties.

Civil Administration

While the police, the fire department and the military are reporting in groups to the Control Headquarters, the Civil Administration should gradually take over control of operations. Till the civil administration is in place, the police and the military should carry out the management of the disaster. The District Collector or the District Magistrate as per the appointment in that district will head the civil administration. However, it may be possible that the District Collector and his staff or their families have become the initial casualties. There is therefore a requirement for two to three districts to be clubbed together so that they can provide mutual support to each other. For such eventualities the District Collector and his staff should familiarise themselves with the district in which they will have to set up control headquarters, if required.

Civil Defence Organisation

Civil Defence Organisations of the district will have to be pressed into service at the earliest, while the police and military cordon off the area, provide protection to the medical teams and control the movement of the public, ascertain the nature of disaster and commence its mitigation. The civil defence organisation personnel will be mainly responsible to collect the dead at selected places, help in evacuating the serious casualties to places where immediate medical help is available, locate the minor casualties at places where they can be observed by medical personnel etc. In other words, they will have to be in close contact with the casualties. However, unlike other disasters (where the danger of contamination is not there) the people rendering relief will have to be properly equipped with and protected against contamination. There is a need therefore, for civil defence organisations in each district to have NBC protective equipment. Due to the short life span of NBC equipment and their high cost, it may not be possible to have these stored in every district of the country. It is therefore recommended that the civil defence organisations in the major cities and more vulnerable districts, like cities and towns having chemical industries or nuclear installations should be equipped with NBC protective equipment. This should include disposable NBC suits and minimum individual protective equipment. A pack of approximately 100 sets should be adequate to meet the immediate requirements. Subsequently, based on the magnitude of the disaster, NBC protective equipment from the adjacent districts or states could also be moved in.

Non-Government Organisations (NGOs)

NGOs will also have an important role to play in the management of chemical disasters. However, since they will possibly not have any training to operate with NBC protective equipment, nor will they have any NBC protective equipment in their possession, they will be best employed in tasks, which are out of the contaminated area and away from contaminated personnel. In fact as far as possible they should not be permitted to enter the cordon established around the area of disaster by the police and the military. Once adequate protective equipment is available they could be used to equip personnel from NGOs so that they could also be employed for various relief tasks.

Sequence of Action for Management of Chemical Disasters

Sequence of action for disaster management will be contingent upon the time, place, population of the area, type of chemical, whether the disaster is caused due to an accident or sabotage or a deliberate act of chemical attack by terrorists. In case it is by terrorists, then there may be a possibility of certain delayed explosions also, particularly when the various organisations are attempting to mitigate the disaster. This factor must be taken into consideration while planning the management of the chemical disaster. A possible sequence of action could be:

- The "First Responders" call up the police and fire department at the earliest at telephone numbers 100 and 101 (these numbers are for New Delhi; other places may have different numbers).
- By the time the police arrive on the scene there is likely to be a rush of people running away from the site of disaster. While establishing road blocks it may not be possible to convince all the people that their welfare lies in remaining within the cordon and out of the area of influence of the disaster. Police should set up the Control Headquarters in a direction opposite to the direction of the wind, preferably in a building so that it has inherent protection from the fumes of the chemical agent. They should also reconnoiter covered places and buildings that can be used for establishing Medical Aid Posts and for Chemical Decontamination Centres. It must be ensured that the police (men and women) have necessary NBC protection kits. They could announce through loud hailers, for people to assemble near the police control room and await the arrival of medical help. The police should also announce, asking people to wash the exposed parts of their bodies with water and soap, or scrub the exposed parts of their bodies with common earth and mud. These would help in adsorbing the chemical agents that could otherwise penetrate through the skin, even if they are in gaseous form. The unaffected people should assist the police in segregating the serious casualties. All people affected or otherwise must remain in the area so that they can be observed

by the medical teams for any contamination and render medical help.

- The fire fighting and military personnel who would have reported to the Control Headquarters would set up decontamination points for the casualties, to wash the eyes and face and exposed portion of the hands etc thoroughly with water, and if possible with soap and water.
- The medical authorities would inform the hospitals which have geared up to accept the chemical casualties. It must be understood that sending chemical exposure casualties to hospitals/nursing homes which are not geared up to receive the casualties are likely to cause greater casualties because they would contaminate the patients and medical staff who would not have taken the necessary precautions.
- Combined fire service, police and military teams would also proceed to the source of disaster to ascertain the type of chemical that has caused the disaster, and try to seal the source. For example, if it is a persistent chemical agent spilled over an area, they could cover it up with earth, cordon off and mark the area for deliberate action to be carried out subsequently, to remove the persistent agent from the area. The type of chemical, the quantity etc. should be intimated to the Control Headquarters for onward transmission to the medical authorities for establishing the nature of treatment to be meted out to the casualties, as also the type and quantities of medicines required. This team should also make a tentative assessment of the number of people affected and intimate the same to the Control Headquarters, so that decision may be taken whether

help is required from the neighbouring districts or states. The magnitude of the disaster will also indicate whether national assistance has to be called for, and arrangements made to receive and deploy the same without wastage of time. An important task of the police accompanying these teams would be to protect the personnel from the casualties who may try to snatch protective equipment in order to protect themselves against the chemicals. If possible, they should try to apprehend suspicious personnel or terrorists in the area who may be responsible for the chemical disaster. An indication of such terrorists would be personnel in the area who are equipped with the protective equipment and may or may not be carrying weapons to protect themselves in case they are apprehended. It is essential, therefore, for some of the police personnel to be equipped with weapons. The balance of the police personnel should carry with them bamboo or fibreglass shields and sticks to protect themselves.

- The medical personnel who would have arrived should be divided into two major groups supported by the police, military, fire fighting and civil defence personnel. The strength will depend upon the availability of NBC protective equipment. One group composed of small teams should operate in the near vicinity of the Control Headquarters and set up a medical aid post in the building or area selected by the Control Headquarters. The personnel who have been blocked by the police cordon will be provided the initial treatment here, and if no treatment is required may be kept under observation for some time. The second group will be formed into teams to move towards the source of disaster. Depending upon the number of personnel and protective equipment available these teams should be formed. A suggested grouping of the team is given in Table 4.3.

1.	Doctor	-	1
2.	Nursing Assistant with medical relief	-	4
3.	Police/military protection	-	4
4.	Photographer with camera	-	1
5.	Stretcher-bearers with five stretchers and ten casualty bags and white sheets. (These casualty bags are to be replenished when the casualties are carried to the Control Centre)	-	10

Table 4.3 Composite Teams for Disaster Area.

The casualties are likely to be of four types: Less affected and capable of walking; greatly affected but not in a position to walk; severely affected in critical condition and lastly the dead. As the teams move towards the source of disaster, the less affected persons, particularly those who are in a position to walk will be directed by the doctor to move to the Medical Aid Post set up near the Control Headquarters. The highest priority for evacuation will be given to the severely affected persons. The persons will be indicated by the doctor and if possible provided with medical assistance. A red identification card with the particulars of the person will be tied around his wrist with a chord (the identification card should not be pinned to the clothes because it may be discarded while discarding the contaminated clothes).

In case the person is not in a state to tell his particulars then help will be taken from persons nearby, if possible. In any case the photographer (if possible) should take a photograph for subsequent identification. The person will then be placed in a casualty bag and carried to the Medical Aid Post on a stretcher. The stretcher-bearers will hand over the casualty and return to the team as early as possible. Next in priority for evacuation will be the greatly affected persons who are not in a position to walk. The identification of such people will be with yellow identification cards, and action as taken in the case of severely affected person will be taken. At this stage no action need be taken by this team to evacuate the dead. Once the doctor is certain that the person is not alive, attempt will be made to obtain his identity from persons nearby and the same written on an identification card. In case he cannot be identified, the card will be filled as "NOT IDENTIFIED", and photograph of the person taken. In case the body is lying in an awkward place like centre of a road, then it should be shifted on to a pavement and covered with white cloth, if possible. Depending upon the magnitude of the disaster and the number of persons affected, these teams are likely to be overworked and will have to be replaced or reinforced with additional personnel.

- The people who have reported to the Medical Aid Post should be given medical treatment as required, and kept under observation for late symptoms, if any. They should be advised to wash the exposed surfaces of their body immediately and try and cover the uncovered portion of their bodies.
- The Fire Department should establish ad hoc shower bath, separately for men and women and make provision of soap and if possible some change of clothes.

- The people should have a shower, thoroughly scrubbing themselves with soap and water. As far as possible they should remove all their clothes and dump them in an area earmarked by the fire department personnel. Once they have showered they should drape themselves with fresh clothes for which provision has to be made by the Control Headquarters. In case a change of clothes is not available, it must be remembered that it is better to keep the partially contaminated clothing on, than to be bare bodied. In fact, in such circumstances the people should only wash their hands and face thoroughly and await arrival of fresh clothes before a body shower is taken.

- The Control Headquarters should muster ambulance vehicles from all sources. The drivers and nursing assistants of these ambulances should have NBC protective equipment. The ambulances will lift the casualties from the areas earmarked for them by the Control Headquarters (ambulance park) and take them to the nominated hospitals and report back to the Control Headquarters.

- Teams composed of armed forces and fire department personnel who have instruments like the chemical agent detection and alarm systems, chemical agent monitors and gas chromatographs should proceed downwind from the area of disaster and identify areas that have been affected. The downwind effect will reduce as one moves further from the source of disaster, but would simultaneously spread sideways. These teams should keep monitoring till the level of contamination is within permissible limits. They must continuously relay to the Control Headquarters the areas that are affected so that the broadcasting teams may inform the public accordingly. It should also be possible for these teams to directly inform the broadcasting teams so that the disaster message and the precautions to be taken can be passed without any delay. These teams will also be responsible to give an 'all clear' signal when the safety level of contamination is reached.

- Broadcasting teams composed of civil defence personnel should make announcements regarding the disaster in the areas of the disaster as well as the direction in which the wind is likely to have carried the chemicals. The announcements should include advice to the personnel regarding actions that should be taken by them. Some of the issues that require to be broadcast are:
  - A chemical disaster has taken place in 'X' area.
  - Due to the wind direction the people in 'A', 'B', 'C' areas are likely to be affected.
  - All windows and doors should be shut to make the house as airtight as possible.
  - Move indoors and inside shelters if in these areas.
  - If not in these areas then do not come to these areas.
  - Do not move outdoors.
  - Cover all foodstuffs and water. In case there are any exposed foodstuffs, the same should be disposed of properly so that any human or animal does not consume them inadvertently.
  - Wash with water and soap, particularly the exposed parts of the body.

- The media has a very important role to play at this stage. Large number of people driving cars are tuned to FM channels on the car radio. Personnel at home may be tuned to the television or the FM channels on radio. It would be ideal to broadcast to the public, particularly the following:
  - Occurrence of the disaster.
  - Place of occurrence.
  - The direction in which the wind is blowing the contaminated air and the names of places that are likely to be affected.
  - Not to come to the areas indicated and to move out of these areas as early as possible.
  - To go indoors and remain indoors till "all clear" message is received.
  - To cover their face with a cloth, preferably wet.
  - To shut all the doors and windows and seal them to the best of their ability against outside air entering the house.
  - Cover food and water.
  - Wash exposed parts of the body thoroughly with soap and water and cover them.
- The dead have to be cleared and disposed of with honour and respect and have to be accounted for as well. A conscious decision has to be taken to cremate the bodies rather than burying or following other forms of disposal like immersing in rivers. The bodies will retain the contamination for a long time and hence methods other than cremating by burning are not recommended. As available in certain cities, provision

of electric crematoriums should be made in more towns and cities, because in the case of mass casualties electric crematoriums will be more practicable than the funeral pyre made with wood etc. Teams from the civil defence and volunteers from NGOs donning proper protective equipment should be tasked to collect the dead left covered by white sheets in the area of disaster, at a place nominated by the Control Headquarters.

It is very important that the bodies are identified before they are taken away. A doctor must be available at the place where the bodies are collected to recheck and sign the "death certificate". The bodies should then be put into body bags and taken to the nominated crematorium. The Control Headquarters with the help of the media should broadcast the names of the people who have died, and request their relatives to come directly to the crematorium and give permission for the cremation to be carried out. A time limit of about twelve hours could be given. Some of the actions that,could be taken by the Civil Defence and the NGOs at the crematorium are as follows:

- Make available religious preachers of all religions to conduct the last rites. This could be arranged by NGOs.
- Make provision for wood in case electric crematorium is not available. This may be required since the casualties are expected to be high. This could also be done by NGOs.
- Create a temporary morgue for the bodies that have not been identified. Photographs of such people taken at the place of disaster could be flashed on the television. The temporary morgue could be set up by the civil defence organisation in the area of the crematorium.

- Cremation of the bodies should be prioritised. This could be done by an organisation set up by Civil Defence and NGOs to ensure that the cremations take place without much delay. The bodies that have been identified should be cremated first. The organisation handling the cremation should ensure that a proper record of the bodies along with their photographs is maintained. Officials from the "Office of Birth and Death Registration" should be members of this organisation so that the actions to be taken in such cases are expedited.

Summary of Actions to be taken by Various Agencies

Local Population (First Responders)

- Direct the people to move away from the site of disaster in a direction opposite to the direction of the prevailing wind.
- Inform the police and the fire department for help.
- Intimate regarding the nature of the contaminant and characteristics, if any.
- Intimate the symptoms of the casualties.
- Advise people to cover their faces with wet cloth.
- Advise the people to cover the exposed portions of their body and scrub them with earth or mud.
- Advise the people to wash their eyes, face and exposed parts of the body with soap and water.
- Advise people to get undercover.
- Assist in segregating serious casualties.
- Assist the more affected people to take off their clothes and scrub them with soap and water.

Local Police

- Inform all concerned.
- Establish roadblocks.
- Set up control headquarters opposite to the direction of the prevailing wind.
- Reconnoiter covered places and buildings for establishing medical aid posts and decontamination points.
- Announce using loud hailers to assemble near the police control headquarters and await arrival of medical help.
- Advise people to wash their eyes, face and exposed parts of their body or scrub the exposed parts with common earth or mud if water is not available.
- Protect teams going to the area of disaster from the people affected by the disaster.
- Try to apprehend suspicious persons who may be responsible for the disaster, namely, terrorists.
- Try to ascertain the cause of the disaster and inform the control headquarters.
- Ensure that casualties are photographed and identification tags attached where feasible.

District Authorities

- Direct the RRT to dispatch reconnaissance parties to the site of the disaster.
- Obtain an assessment of the disaster from the reconnaissance parties.
- Seek external help if required.
- Provide early warning to neighbouring districts so that they are prepared if help is sought.

- Contact the armed forces in the station and requisition them if required.
- Contact the other government and non-government agencies for assistance.
- Contact the media and request them to communicate to the general public the actions they should take to protect themselves as well as to assist in the mitigation of the disaster.
- Proceed to the site of disaster to set up the control headquarters and take over control of the situation.

Armed Forces

- Send out reconnaissance parties at the earliest opportunity to assess the situation.
- Assist the local police in setting up cordons and control headquarters.
- In conjunction with fire fighting department set up decontamination points.
- Teams formed in conjunction with the fire department personnel should proceed to the site of disaster and try to seal the source, if possible.
- Try to ascertain the cause of the disaster and intimate to the control headquarters.
- Intimate the control headquarters of the type of chemical and symptoms of the casualties.
- Make a tentative assessment of the casualties and intimate the same to the control headquarters.
- Protect teams going to the disaster area from the affected personnel.
- Try to apprehend suspicious persons in the area in conjunction with the police.

- Ensure that casualties are photographed and identification tags attached.
- In conjunction with the fire department, discern the areas upto which (downwind) the disaster has affected.
- Give all-clear signal at the appropriate time to the control headquarters.

Fire Fighting Department

- Set up decontamination points.
- Set up containers for keeping discarded contaminated clothes during full body decontamination.
- Create soakage pits for the contaminated water.
- Provide soap or detergent to the people for washing.
- Teams formed in conjunction with the military should proceed to the site of the disaster and try and seal the source, if possible.
- Intimate the type of chemical and symptoms of casualties to the control headquarters.
- Make a tentative assessment of the casualties.
- Shift bodies lying at awkward places to safer places.
- In conjunction with the military discern the disaster affected downwind area.
- Intimate the control headquarters once the level of contamination is below danger level.

Medical Authorities

- Intimate the hospitals earmarked for chemical casualty treatment to be prepared to accept contaminated chemical casualties.

- Inform the police control headquarters of the hospitals where the casualties are to be sent and their number.
- Set up medical aid post in the vicinity of the control headquarters in conjunction with the police, military and civil defence organisation.
- Provide first aid to the casualties who have arrived near the control headquarters.
- Pacify and place the remaining persons who are apparently not affected under observation.
- Doctors to coordinate with the police, military, fire service and civil defence people to:
  - Direct those who are less affected and can walk, to the medical aid post.
  - Direct the severely affected people to be carried on stretchers to the nominated hospital.
  - Cover the dead with white cloth.
- Ensure that photographs of the severe casualties and the dead are taken.
- Place identification tags on the casualties and the dead.
- Ensure availability of ambulances at the control headquarters.
- Shift the casualties from the site of disaster to the hospital.

Civil Defence Organisation and NGOs

- Assist in setting up the medical aid posts.
- Assist the fire department in setting up decontamination points and make provision of water, soap and fresh clothes.

- Assist the police, military and fire department in mitigation of the disaster.
- Make announcements of the disaster and the preventive measures to be taken by the people.
- Give all-clear signal at an appropriate time.
- Collect the dead at a central location.
- Ensure proper identification of the dead is done and death certificates are issued.
- Help in moving the dead bodies to the crematorium.
- Organise the presence of religious preachers of all religions at the crematorium to conduct the last rites.
- Make provision for wood in case electric crematorium is not available in the vicinity.
- Create a temporary morgue for unidentified bodies in the general area of the crematorium.
- Cremate the bodies in order of priority.

Media

- Make announcements on television and FM channel of radios intimating the people of the disaster area as well as the precautions they should take.
- Flash frequent intermittent visuals on TV, to create awareness among the public regarding the actions to be taken.
- Broadcast the areas, which are likely to be affected by the downwind.
- Flash on the television the photographs of the unidentified bodies.

- Broadcast the list of people who have been sent to various hospitals, or who have been sent to the crematorium, requesting the kith and kin to reach there for identification.
- Broadcast the all-clear signal when received.

Conclusion

Emergency response plans have to be devised at all levels, viz., industry, locality, region or district, state and the country as a whole. The very nature, complexity, and multi-dimensional impact of chemical disasters require a multi-sectoral and multi-disciplinary approach in planning emergency response action. Success of any response action is a measure of the effectiveness of preparedness planning undertaken at all levels.

The specific character of accidental releases and the magnitude of their off-site impact on public health and the environment, makes emergency response a joint venture of the police, military, civil defence organisations, medical authorities, fire department, media, voluntary agencies and last but not the least the community leaders and local public. Communication is the most vital element in all phases and hence the information support at the site must be prompt, precise and reliable. Communication is essential not only within the network of the emergency response system, but also with the public and the media.

The steps taken in the first few minutes of a chemical accident or man-made disaster such as containment, cordoning off the area, neutralisation of effect etc. will determine the effectiveness of mitigation. The response action has to be mediated by a well-coordinated agency to oversee various inter-departmental efforts at every step. It is essential that the various agencies are equipped with NBC protective equipment so that they themselves do not become casualties while attempting to mitigate the disaster.

5

Management of Nuclear and Radiological Disasters

The nuclear weapon was first used during the Second World War against Japan by the United States of America and the first bomb was dropped over Shima Hospital of Hiroshima on 6 Aug 1945. The device exploded in the air at a height of about 1670 feet from the earth and yielded 12.5 kilotons of energy (one kiloton of energy would cause a water body 1 metre deep, 10 metres wide and 100 metres long to evaporate). The second device was dropped at Nagasaki on 8 Aug 1945 that was exploded at a height of about 1640 feet from the earth and yielded 22 kilotons of energy. Fifty per cent of all deaths were due to burns and about 67 per cent deaths occurred on the first day. Thirty per cent people received lethal doses of radiation. Those who survived within a radius of half a mile of the explosion died in a week or two.

Witnessing the horrendous effects, nuclear bombs have not been used since by any country, though the number of nuclear weapons countries like America and erstwhile USSR or the present-day Russia have, is more than adequate to destroy the world many times over. Global experience of the use of nuclear weapons is confined to the two that were dropped on Japan. Our understanding of the effects of these weapons on cities and their populations is based on studies of Hiroshima and Nagasaki. Casualties of Hiroshima and Nagasaki are shown in Table 5.1.

Zone	Population	Killed	Injured
	HIROSHIMA		
0 -1 km	31,200	26,700	3,000
1- 2.5 km	144,000	39,600	53,000
2.5 - 5 km	80,000	1,700	20,000
Total	**2,56,000**	**68,000**	**76,000**
	NAGASAKI		
0-1 km	30,900	27,700	1,900
1 - 2.5 km	27,300	9,500	1,300
2.5 - 5 km	115,200	1,300	11,000
Total	**1,73,800**	**38,000**	**21,000**

Table 5.1 Casualties at Hiroshima and Nagasaki.

The use of nuclear weapons during a war cannot be ruled out totally, particularly on the pretext of "ending the war" or saving the "honour and prestige" of the country. From the consideration of economics too, nuclear devices are less expensive as compared to the cost of the quantity of munitions, the number of air sorties and the field force required. However, the possibility of use of nuclear weapons by any country, when no war has been declared is remote though the possibility of using various forms of derivates of nuclear devices by terrorists and non-state actors remains.

Nuclear Capability of Terrorists

There is a feeling among people that with the availability of scientific and technological information and fissionable material in the black market a crude nuclear bomb would not be difficult to assemble. This feeling may not be well placed because if that were true, then many more countries than the present eight would have had nuclear weapons. The case of Libya not being able to develop nuclear weapons is a case in point. Hence, development of nuclear bomb by terrorist groups or non-state actors can be considered a relatively distant possibility. What may be of greater concern is as per General Alexander Lebed, the former Russian National Security Chief, approximately 100 nuclear devices of suitcase size are missing from the Russian stockpile. These could pose a grave danger if they were to land in the hands of terrorists or fanatics. In addition, radiological weapons, although not as destructive as nuclear weapons, also pose a serious danger, particularly as a terrorist threat. These are weapons that use conventional explosives, such as dynamite, to disperse radioactive materials, including the highly radioactive waste material from nuclear power reactors or other non-weapon sources. These could be produced relatively easily and therefore may be attractive weapons for terrorists. With the concept of 'suicide bombers' and 'jehadis' involved in terrorist activities, a simple form of creating a radiological disaster would be by attacking the industries having radioactive waste materials. The main problem in such cases would be to penetrate through the safeguards.

To be able to mitigate nuclear disasters it is essential for the general population to have a broad understanding of their characteristics and how these weapons affect men and materials.

Effects of Nuclear Explosion

A number of characteristic phenomena, some visible, some not apparent, occur during a nuclear explosion. Nuclear weapon detonation is accompanied with the release of a huge quantity of energy, which is transformed into blast waves, heat and nuclear radiations. A sharp and bright flash of light also generally accompanies it. A fireball forms, which grows rapidly in size and ascends fast. Photographs of the mushroom cloud forming are shown in Figures 5.1 and 5.2.

A large luminous spherical wave surrounds the fireball (the luminance is apparently from the electronically excited oxygen atoms produced by the shock wave passing through the low density air). As the fireball touches the earth during its rapid growth, it causes intense heat. Where the fireball touches the earth's surface, a crater is formed as a result of vaporisation of soil. The size of the crater varies with the height of the explosion as well as the yield of the device. Some rock and soil in the area vaporise and are sucked into the fireball. Some more materials melt either completely or on their surfaces and the strong afterwinds cause large amount of dirt, dust and other particles to be sucked up as the fireball rises. The radioactive cloud rises before spreading out abruptly into a mushroom-like formation. A land surface bursts where the device explodes on the ground or close to the ground is shown in Figure 5.3.

Fig 5.1 Formation of the Mushroom Cloud

Fig 5.2 Formation of the Mushroom Cloud

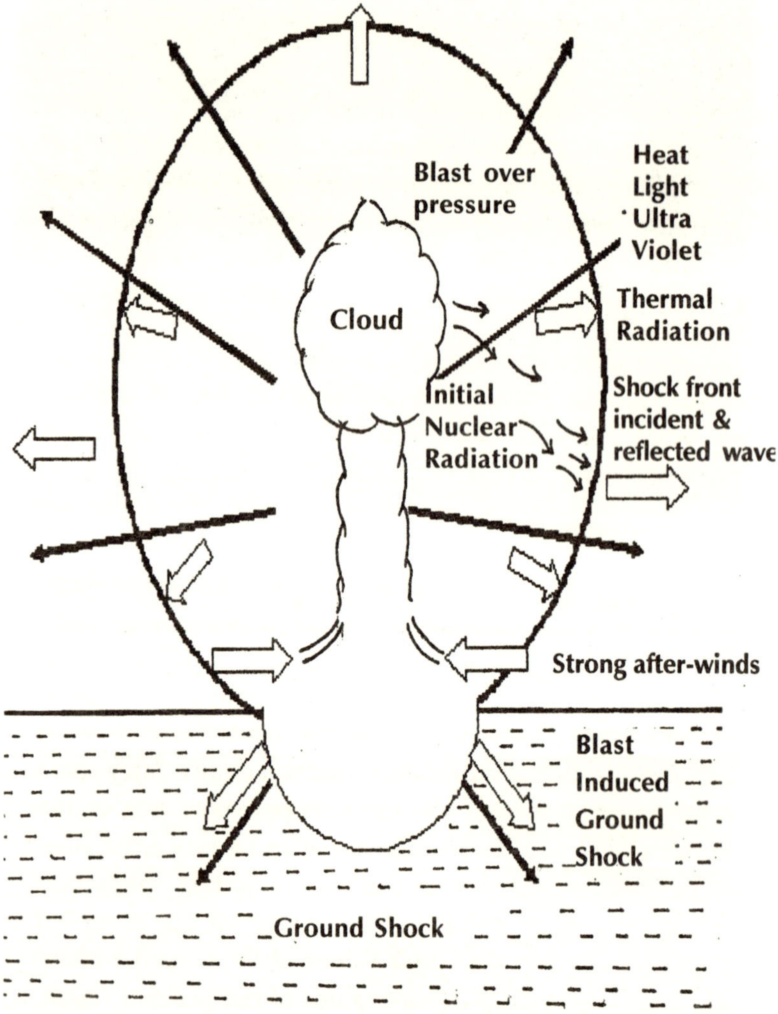

Fig 5.3 A Land Surface Burst

The initial devastating phase lasts for about 10-90 seconds. Whatever survives after the destructive initial phase shall have to overcome the effects of ionising radiations for survival. The distribution of energy after a nuclear blast is shown in Figure 5.4.

Fifty per cent of the energy in nuclear explosion is converted into blast wave. However, it causes approximately 35 per cent casualties. The thermal and nuclear injuries contribute 50 per cent and 15 per cent respectively as depicted in Figure 5.5.

Blast

A fraction of a second after a nuclear explosion, a high-pressure wave forms and it moves outwards from the centre of the fireball. It is initiated by quick expansion of hot gases produced in the nuclear explosion. The front of the blast wave travels very rapidly behaving like a wall of compressed air. This wall or shock front, where the energy is moving at a speed many times that of sound, causes intense damage. It causes few primary casualties to men, as the human body is very resistant to overpressure. Collapsing buildings, flying glass and debris, will cause most of the casualties. Human beings may be blown away due to the blast and high wind speeds and levelled against objects and structures. After some time the pressure behind the front drops below that of the surrounding atmosphere and the negative phase of the blast wave commences. During this phase, a partial vacuum is produced and the air instead of being pushed out is sucked in causing afterwinds. The peak values of the negative phase are much smaller than the peak values of the positive phase. At the end of the negative phase the atmosphere returns to ambient pressure.

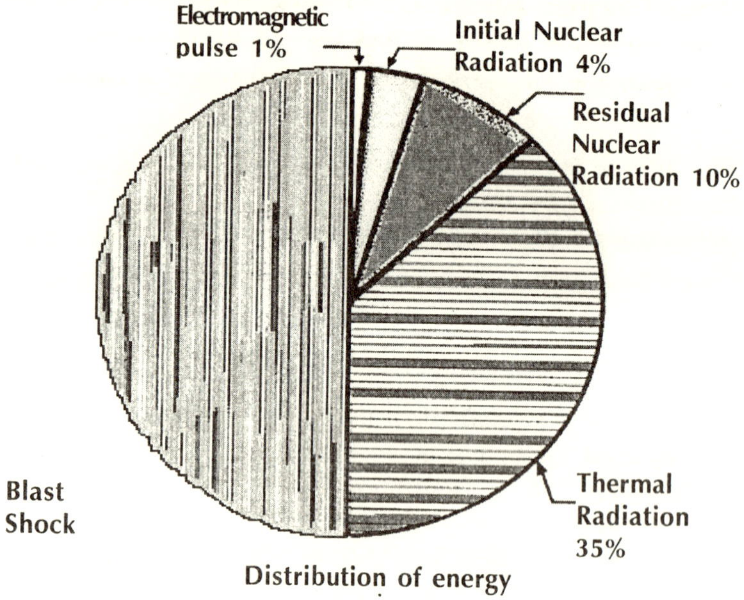

Fig 5.4 Distribution of Energy after Nuclear Explosion.

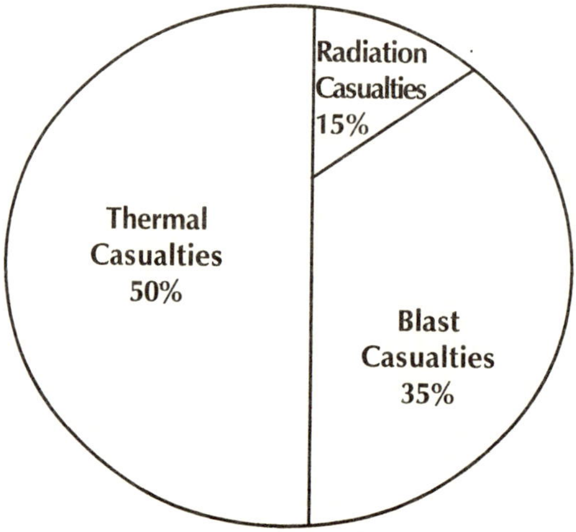

Fig 5.5 Casualty Distribution following Nuclear Explosion.

The blast causes very large number of fatal casualties due to physical injuries. In addition, for those who survive, various organs are likely to be affected. The most sensitive organ of man to blast wave is the eardrum. The other sensitive organs to blast wave are lungs, gastrointestinal tract, blood vessels, and body joints. Very large number of people will have burst eardrums, though there is likely to be lesser casualties due to damage to heart and lungs because of the resilience of the rib cage.

Heat

The diameter of the fireball as a result of airburst of a 20 kiloton weapon will be approximately 220 metres, which is achieved in less than a millionth of a second. The fireball temperature soon after the burst when measured from ground is about 8000°C. The temperature of the fireball falls steadily with time. The extent of injury or damage caused by thermal radiation or the chance of igniting combustible material depends to a large extent upon the amount of thermal radiation energy received by a unit area of skin, fabric or other exposed material within the short interval of time. The most important physical effects of the high temperatures resulting from the absorption of thermal radiation are burning of skin, scorching, charring and ignition of combustible substances.

On exposure to a nuclear explosion, casualties from burns may easily exceed those from any other causes. The burns may be caused directly by thermal radiation from the fireball (flash burns) or indirectly as a result of fire caused by the radiation (flame burns). The latter are identical with burns caused by any large fire. Burns are classified according to their severity in terms of depth of injury as follows:

- **First degree**: Redness of the skin.
- **Second degree:** Injury is deeper with blistered skin.
- **Third degree:** The whole thickness of the skin is destroyed sometimes along with deeper tissue.

A further grading is used, in that, within each class the burns may be mild, moderate or severe. The medical effects of a burn on the individual are determined not only by the depth of the injury but also by the area of the body surface, which is affected. Thus, a first-degree burn over the whole body may well be much more serious than a third degree burn at one spot.

The thermal wave or heat flash contains about a third of the total energy released by a nuclear bomb and is of short duration of a few seconds. At Hiroshima and Nagasaki the heat was sufficient to burn exposed human skin at distances as great as 4 km from Ground Zero (GZ), which is the spot on the ground surface vertically beneath or above which a nuclear weapon has exploded. The greatest damage of all kinds occurs at GZ. Many people caught in the open within about 1.2 km from ground zero were burnt to death; others who were closer just evaporated.

The thermal radiation on the eyes causes flash blindness and permanent retinal scarring. The initial brilliant flash causes flash blindness. Individuals gazing in the direction of fireball will suffer the maximum. Reflected light from clouds and objects in the field of view, may also affect personnel who were not looking in the direction of the fireball. During the day flash blindness generally does not persist for more than two minutes. At night, it may last for 15-30 minutes because the pupils are dilated and more flash energy falls on the retina. A retinal burn resulting in permanent damage from scarring is also caused by the concentration of direct thermal energy on the retina by the lens. This occurs only when the fireball is actually in the individual's field of vision. Slight burns will heal completely but those, which are more severe, can cause permanent damage and blind spots on the retina. Complete loss of vision will, however, be a rarity. It has been estimated that only 2 to 3 per cent of flash casualties will have retinal burns and very few of these will suffer complete or partial blindness.

In Hiroshima 20-30 percent of the casualties were due to flash burns. This type of casualty figure was high because most of the population was in the open at the time of the attack. Most of those who suffered flame burns did not survive because they were caught in the burning buildings and could not escape. Second degree burns were healed within four weeks but more severe burns were infected.

Nuclear Radiation

About 15 per cent of the energy yield of a nuclear explosion is given off as ionising radiation. The response of an individual to nuclear radiation depends on the total amount of radiation received, the unrecovered damage from doses received previously, individual body tolerance, injury received simultaneously with dose of radiation and the length of time during which the total radiation is received. The radiation-absorbed dose is measured in rads and is taken as the unit of radiation absorbed by the body. The acceptable exposure to human beings while working in a radiologically contaminated area is as follows:

- Negligible Risk - 5 Rads
- Moderate Risk - 20 Rads
- Emergency Risk - 50 Rads.
- Total dose should not exceed in 30 days - 75 Rads.

The effects of nuclear radiation on the human body are given at Table 5.2.

Rad Dose/Rads	Effects
Upto 150	No short-term effect.
150-250	Nausea and vomiting within 3-6 hours and lasts upto 24 hours
250-350	Nausea and vomiting within 1-6 hours, lasting 1-2 days. Symptoms reappear after 1-2 weeks and last upto 6 weeks. Upto 30% deaths occur.
350-600	Nausea and vomiting within 1-6 hours, lasting 1-2 days. Symptoms reappear after 1-4 weeks and last upto 8 weeks. 30 -90 % deaths occur in 2-12 weeks.
600-1000	Nausea and vomiting in 30 minutes, lasting 2 days. 90 -100 % deaths occur in 1-6 weeks.
100-2500	Nausea and vomiting in 5-30 minutes. 100% death in 4-14 days.
More than 2500	Nausea and vomiting almost immediately. 100 % death in 1-2 days

Table 5.2 Effects of Nuclear Radiation Exposure.

Nuclear radiation can be divided into two categories, viz., initial and residual. Initial radiation is the quantity of radiation received within one minute from the time of explosion. The initial radiation dose at GZ in Hiroshima was of the order of 100,000 Rads. Residual radiation consists of induced radiation and the fallout. The induced radiation is limited to the area around GZ. However, the fallout, consisting of fission products and debris sucked up in the mushroom cloud, can contaminate a very large area depending on the weather conditions. The residual radiation will continue to pose radiation hazard till it decays.

Radiation injuries can arise from the immediate burst of gamma and neutron radiations created in the explosion, or the radiation from fallout. The major hazard is from gamma rays in the radioactive fallout, but beta rays and even alfa particles can contribute to the radiation exposure when the radioactive material is deposited on the body, ingested or inhaled. In nuclear disasters the chances of nuclear radiation effect along with other injuries like burns, cuts etc. are common. Such combined injuries lead to infection. Infection is second only to head injury as the cause of death.

Delayed or late effects may appear months or years after irradiation and include a wide variety of effects in almost all tissues and organs. Some of the possible delayed effects are:

- **Life shortening** may take place as a result of a number of factors, like decreased immunity, damage to connective tissues, premature ageing etc.
- **Cataract formation** was first detected after five years in Hiroshima and Nagasaki.
- **Chronic radiodermatis** causing delayed irreversible changes of the skin.

- **Leukaemia** was expected and found among Hiroshima and Nagasaki survivors. Peak incidence occurred six years after exposure. Children who were exposed to radiation when they were less than ten years of age were found almost twice as susceptible to leukaemia as older individuals.
- **Cancer** of thyroid, lungs, breast and gastrointestinal systems were noticed in Japan. The type of cancer depends on the area irradiated, dose, age etc.

Radioactive fallout depends on the size of the nuclear bomb and the height of its burst from the ground. Local fallout takes place depositing the nuclear material downwind and exposing people within the first 24 hours. Such fallout constitutes about half of the total radioactivity produced by explosion. The other half, containing finer particles, rises with the mushroom cloud into the atmosphere and spreads over vast areas around the globe, differing in intensity. Inhalation of radioactive dust from the fallout can result in the internal radioactive contamination affecting the lungs. If the dose is high enough, actual local effects even leading to death may occur, apart from long term effects such as fibrosis and cancer. It is possible that the radioactive products of the bomb may be inhaled with contaminated air or ingested with contaminated food or water.

Effects of a Nuclear Attack on a Medium Sized Town

To study the effects of a nuclear blast, a typical medium sized town has been considered whose population is approximately 3 million people. The spread of this population from the centre has been taken as follows:

- Within 1 km 20% (6,00,000)
- Between 1 to 2 km 30% (9,00,000)
- Between 2 to 3 km 25% (7,50,000)
- Within 4 kms 25% (7,50, 000)

Based on a United Nations study on nuclear weapons, the following yardstick has been adopted and depicted in Figure 5.6:

* Within 1 km radius from the GZ, all buildings will be destroyed and 95 per cent of those inhabiting the area will be casualties (dead or seriously injured).
* Between 1 to 2 km from GZ, there will be partial or complete destruction of buildings and 50 per cent of those inhabiting the area will be casualties.
* Between 2 to 3 km from GZ, there will be heavy destruction to buildings and about 35 per cent of the inhabitants will be casualties.

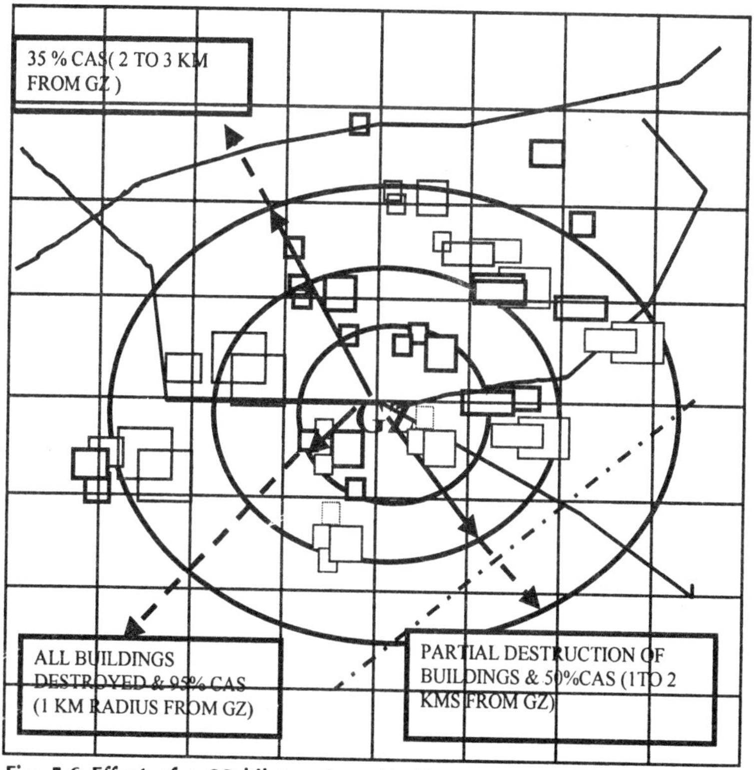

Fig. 5.6 Effect of a 20 kiloton Low Air Burst on a Medium Size Town

The likely details of casualties (zone wise) is given in Table 5.3. During peak traffic time such as prior to and after office hours, the casualties may be much more. At normal times a 20 kiloton nuclear bomb is likely to cause 1.3 million casualties (out of the 3 million population) of which 0.5 million will take place immediately and 0.8 million over a period of time.

	Less than 1 km	1 km to 2 km	2 km to 3 km
Population Spread	20% 6 lakhs	30% 9 lakhs	25% 7.5 lakhs
Damage Effect	All buildings destroyed. 95 % casualties	Partial/complete destruction of buildings. 50% casualties	Destruction of buildings. 35% casualties.
Casualties	5,85,000	4,50,000	2,62,500
Total Casualty 1.3 Million approximately			

Table 5.3 Casualties likely to be caused by a 20 Kiloton Bomb in a Medium Sized Town

Scene of a Nuclear Disaster

There will be an extremely bright flash of light, several times brighter than the sun, dazzling personnel and causing temporary loss of sight or retinal burns. This will be accompanied by release of intense heat and followed shortly by a thunderous sound of a blast. Soon a huge ball of fire brighter than the sun will be seen rising towards the sky. Gradually, this ball of fire would transform into a mushroom-like cloud. People far away from the site of the incident will be able to see, hear and guess what could have happened.

Persons near the site of the disaster would not be alive to hear or feel anything. In fact many would have simply vapourised. The trauma and shock would be so high that for quite some time the surviving people would be stunned, not knowing what to do.

At the site of the disaster and around, buildings would have collapsed trapping people below the debris; structures would be burning and vehicles would be lying all over upturned and possibly burning. There will be a haze around the site of the disaster as the immediate fallout of the radioactive dust takes place. Trees in the area would have been uprooted and sent like missiles causing secondary damage. The site of the disaster would be terrible to look at, particularly the people who have been injured and traumatised. Burn cases will be very high and the sight of burnt and charred bodies, or persons with their skin and flesh peeling off their bodies will be a familiar sight. The whole area would be in a state of chaos. The almost universal reaction among the survivors will be lethargy, emotional insensitivity, mental weakness and depression rather than panic. Those who are able will walk silently like shadows looking straight ahead with no facial expression or initiative. There will be no organised activity; in most cases, people are likely to be self-centred and think only of their own escape and survival. Severe anxiety will persist for weeks to months. People will be unable to eat, personality changes will take place due to the witnessing of the large number of maimed, and burnt people. It will be a source of trauma for those who escape severe injuries and survive (extracted from experiences of Hiroshima and Nagasaki).

The scene of a nuclear disaster will not only traumatise the persons affected in the area, but is also likely to traumatise the persons who will visit the site for providing succour to the casualties and managing the after-effects of the nuclear disaster.

Preparation for a Nuclear Disaster

There is no doubt that the nation must work out contingencies to face a nuclear disaster. However, the possibility of an attack with a nuclear bomb in the present-day geopolitical scenario is only remotely possible if there is a war and that too when the adversary is likely to face a strategic defeat. However, the possibility of radiological bombs or suitcase bombs (found missing from the stocks of Soviet Russia) falling into the hands of terrorists or attack by terrorists on nuclear installations cannot be ruled out. The possibility of initiating a nuclear disaster by terrorists is much higher than a conventional nuclear attack by another country. The devastating effect of such devices will possibly not be as severe as that of the 20-kiloton bomb described, but the manifestations will remain the same albeit with lesser intensity. In fact, the casualty pattern may also be comparatively less, but far higher than a conventional natural disaster. Disaster mitigation preparedness has, therefore, to cater for all the primary and secondary effects of a nuclear bomb attack.

General Plan of Action

Evidence of a nuclear disaster will travel far and wide, without anyone having to inform the concerned authorities. The flash, bang and fireball will be clear indicators of a nuclear disaster. The type and size of the nuclear device will determine the magnitude of the hazard.

The first and foremost activity would be to set up a Control Headquarters at the district level. However, if the district authorities themselves have become casualty, which is likely to happen, then the adjacent district must set up a Control Headquarters under the leadership of the District Collector/ Commissioner. The Control Headquarters should be composed of personnel from the police, military, fire department, civil defence, medical authorities and NGOs. At the earliest opportunity the Disaster Management Authority at the state level should superimpose itself on the Control Headquarters so that assistance from other districts of the state can be mustered. The state should have the primary responsibility for consequence management of nuclear disasters. The Centre's assistance on consequence management situations will generally be in support of the state's disaster relief efforts, to include efforts in response to a nuclear incident.

The police will have to cordon off the area and ensure that only personnel with NBC protective equipment are permitted to proceed anywhere near the site of disaster. It will also be the responsibility of the police to ensure that the roads leading in and out of the area are kept open for movement of vehicles and ambulances carrying casualties. The military could join the police in maintaining order in the area of disaster. The fire department personnel (mandatory to be equipped with NBC protective equipment) will be given priority of movement into the area so that primary and secondary fires and fires due to electric short-circuiting are put out. The army and police personnel who would possibly be having NBC protective equipment could assist them. Simultaneously, these teams could extricate personnel buried under the rubble of destroyed buildings. The Control Headquarters should depute persons with loud hailers to accompany these teams to the area of disaster, and announce for the casualties to move towards the Control Headquarters. A prominent landmark in the area should be announced and guides placed by the Control Headquarters to direct the personnel to the Medical Aid Post established in the vicinity of the Control Headquarters. The less affected persons will be requested to assist the more affected ones to reach the Medical Aid Post. This will reduce the number of stretcher-borne casualties considerably.

Joint teams composed of doctors and medical personnel, the military, the police, NGOs and personnel from civil defence should move towards the site of disaster in an organised manner. There should be a photographer with camera with this team. The doctors here should do selective segregation or triage. Triage is an essential component of management of casualties and is aimed at the utilisation of available medical resources in a timely and orderly manner, for efficiently instituting medical care and treatment of maximum number of casualties. The triage for nuclear disasters can be prioritised into five categories as follows:

- **Priority I:** Casualties who are unable to walk and require life-saving care within a short time. Such casualties will be evacuated on stretchers directly to the place where ambulances will be parked, to be taken away to the nominated hospitals.
- **Priority II:** Casualties with severe injuries who are in need of major or prolonged surgery and who will require hospitalisation. However, delay of this care will not adversely affect the outcome of the injury. Such casualties will be carried to the Medical Aid Post and provided with emergency medical treatment required. They will be evacuated to the nominated hospitals once the Priority I cases have been evacuated.
- **Priority III:** Casualties who have minor injuries and can be provided medical assistance at the Medical Aid Post itself. Such people may not be evacuated to the hospital for medical treatment. However, they will have to be kept under observation for psychological effects and disorders.
- **Priority IV:** Casualties with severe life-threatening injuries who would not survive with optimal medical care or casualties whose injuries are so severe that

there are no chances of survival. However, since they are still alive they would have to be provided with necessary succour. Such casualties should be brought under a nearby shelter and provided with medical comforts. Since, the medical personnel will be at a premium, personnel from NGOs and Civil Defence Organisations should provide the succour on humanitarian grounds till they breathe their last. This process may take a few hours in certain cases and hence adequate relief and replacements should be organised.

- **Priority V:** These will be casualties who have breathed their last. Doctors should check them and declare them dead. Such bodies should be shifted to an earmarked area, covered with white sheet and guarded by Civil Defence Personnel or NGOs, so that animals and birds do not swarm on the bodies.

Casualty Management

- Photographs of all casualties should be taken, particularly the severely injured who have been evacuated from the site of disaster, the casualties who have no hope of survival and have been left in the area of disaster, and those who are dead.
- An identification tag must be attached around the wrist of the casualty. Pinning on the dress will not be a correct method, because the contaminated clothes will have to be shed thereby possibly causing the identification card to be lost. A sample identification card could have the details as shown in Fig 5.7

Identification Card

Name:
Age: Sex: ***Address with telephone number*** Residence: Office:

Fig. 5.7 Casualty Identification Card.

- The identification cards should be in different colours according to the triage, if possible. For example:

  Priority I - Red Card

  Priority II - Yellow Card

  Priority IV - White Card

The identification card should initially be placed near the face and the photographer should try to capture the details of both the card and the person's face in the same photograph.

- At the Medical Aid Post or the Ambulance Park, wherever the casualties are taken, they should shed their outer clothing and wash and clean the exposed parts of the body. 90 to 95 per cent of radiological decontamination is achieved by removing contaminated clothes. Washing or wiping the exposed surfaces of the face with water and soap should have the casualty 98 per cent decontaminated. Subsequently, the hair should be washed or clipped. In case they are not in a position to do the same themselves, persons from Civil Defence Organisations and NGOs should help the casualties to decontaminate themselves of radiological dust.

- The clothing should be kept in sealed polythene packets and tagged for subsequent disposal by incineration.
- Disposal of wastewater from casualty decontamination needs special attention so as to avoid contamination of groundwater resources. This is easier said than done because in a disaster situation it will be difficult to adhere to the precautions required. The best that can be done in a disaster scenario is to dig a large pit and let the wastewater flow into it. The area should be marked and fenced as hazardous, to be cleared later, positively.

The Media

The media using the FM and television channels is the most effective means of reaching out to the people in a nuclear disaster. The media should:

- Intimate the area of the disaster and advise people to avoid moving towards that area.
- Request NGOs and Civil Defence Organisations to report to the Control Headquarters.
- Advise people to dispose of all open food by burying the same in the earth.
- Request people to send clothes to the Control Headquarters for replacing the contaminated clothing of casualties.

- Display the photographs of the casualties who have been sent to various hospitals, intimating the names of the hospitals.
- Display the photographs of the dead and ask their relatives to come to the crematorium.

Honourable Disposal of the Dead

The dead bodies should be carried to an electric crematorium. It is the safest medium to cremate the dead bodies of a nuclear disaster. Since certain religions do not permit the cremation in normal course, priests of all religions should be available at the crematorium, and be requested to advise the people of the correct manner of honourable disposal. Cremations could also be prioritised. For example, bodies that have been identified and some relatives have arrived at the crematorium should be cremated first. Bodies that have been identified but no relatives have arrived should be cremated next, say within twelve hours. Bodies that have not been identified should be kept in the morgue (to be established) near the crematorium for delayed identification. However, such unidentified bodies may not be kept for more than twenty-four hours, if possible. Photographs in all cases must be taken, and death certificates issued by concerned authorities. Arrangements in the crematorium for the morgue, assembling of priests of all religions, provision of wood in case electric crematorium is not available, ensuring the presence of a photographer, ensuring that the concerned authorities issue the death certificate etc. should be the responsibility of Civil Defence Organisations and NGOs.

The duties and responsibilities of the various agencies have been summarised in the Chapter 4 "Management of Chemical Disasters". Most of the duties are similar in nature, however, due to the difference in the nature of the disaster and therefore its after-effects, mitigation and tackling of the various nuances will vary. For example, buildings will not collapse burying people under the debris in a chemical disaster, whereas the same is most likely to take place in a nuclear disaster. Similarly, the open wounds due to burns and missile hits, which will take place in a nuclear disaster, will not take place in a chemical disaster. The disaster situation and its magnitude will remain hazy for quite some time; moreover, motivating people to surge forward to assist in a nuclear disaster will be difficult particularly if they do not have NBC protective equipment, even when the same may not be very essential. Some of the duties of the various agencies are summarised in the subsequent paragraphs.

Duties and Tasks of Various Agencies

Civil Administration

- Set up Control Headquarters composed of police, military, fire department, medical, civil defence, NGOs and media.
- Set up communication channels with the relevant state departments, hospitals and all concerned.
- In case the local district administration itself has been severely affected by the disaster, then the neighbouring district (as per existing plans) must set up the Control Headquarters.
- Direct the media to make broadcasts without causing panic to ensure dissemination of correct information, divert vehicles and personnel from coming to the area of disaster so that roads are kept open for evacuation of casualties.
- Open a record centre (preferably computerised) for recording the names and details of the casualties.

- Inform the designated hospitals of the number of casualties being dispatched.
- Make provision of ambulances and vehicles to dispose of the dead.

Police

- Cordon off the area.
- Keep the roads clear of incoming and outgoing traffic for induction of assistance and deinduction of casualties.
- Provide armed personnel with the teams going to the disaster area to provide protection.
- Control the movement of people.
- Provide protection and control at the Medical Aid Post, decontamination points, ambulance dispatch areas, dispatch areas of dead bodies, clothing distribution point etc.
- It will be the responsibility of the police to maintain an atmosphere of discipline at all these places.

Armed Forces

- Assist the police in cordoning off the area and maintaining discipline.
- Accompany the teams going to the site of disaster and assist in the retrieval and evacuation of casualties.
- Send teams with radiological detection equipment to record the level of radiation at various places and advise whether rescue teams should go there.
- Monitor the radiation absorbed level of the rescue teams so that they are not endangered by contamination.

- Assist the fire fighting team in rescuing casualties.
- Provide NBC protective equipment, if available, to the people evacuating casualties.

Firefighting

- Put out fires.
- Rescue casualties buried under the debris.
- Assist the medical teams in handling casualties particularly burn casualties.
- Set up decontamination points.

Medical

- Establish Medical Aid Posts and provide medical relief and assistance .
- Form teams and move into the disaster area and carry out triage of casualties.
- Provide medical succour to those casualties who have no chance of survival.
- Assist psychologically disturbed persons.
- Prepare the seriously injured casualties with emergency medical assistance for evacuation to hospitals.
- Ensure that all casualties have identification cards tied around their wrists.
- Ensure that photographs of the casualties are taken.

Media

- Ensure that photographs of all casualties are taken.
- Carry out broadcasts of the disaster and advise the people not to clutter the roads with vehicles. Advise them measures that they should take like disposing of uncovered food etc.

- Telecast the photographs of the casualties on television and inform the location of medical aid post in the disaster area, name of hospital in case evacuated, and place of crematorium in case dead.

Civil Defence and NGOs

It is unlikely that the civil defence and personnel from NGOs will have NBC protective equipment. They should not be permitted to enter the disaster area till NBC protective equipment is received from the military or any other source. They could carry out the following duties:

- Assist in establishing the Control Headquarters.
- Assist in establishing the decontamination points along with the pits for contaminated wastewater.
- Provide medical and moral support to personnel who are not going to survive.
- Evacuate stretcher-borne casualties.
- Arrange for provision of clothes to be given to the casualties after decontamination.

Conclusion

In case of a Nuclear Explosion, the level of disaster will be so great, that it is difficult to appreciate the extent of the disaster. The total Command and Control setup of the Government, may be partially or wholly destroyed, and it may take some time to regain balance, to commence mitigating the disaster. Nuclear-Proof Command and Control centres should be constructed for the protection of important persons; facilities for the protection of the general public should be available for protection against the Radio Active dust, which will keep spreading from the atmosphere, for quite some time. Drills must be practiced, so that people can move into covered places, like the metro railway etc. where available. Storage facility for food and water may also have to be catered for, in such areas.

In page 133 of this book, a brief description of the disaster site, as extracted from the experiences of *Hiroshima* and *Nagasaki* have been given. These were with Atomic Bombs of 12.5 kilotons, and 22 kilotons of energy. These caused casualties, as high as 1,44,000, out of a total population of 2,56,000 in *Hiroshima*, and 59,000, out of a total population of 1,73,800 in *Nagasaki.* With the very high density of population we have, not only in our metropolitan cities, but also in the small towns of our country, and considering the fact that, any Nuclear Weapon used today, is not likely to be less than megaton capacity, one shudders to imagine, what would be the extent of the catastrophe. The multiple injuries, due to Radiation, burns, cuts and broken bones, as well as, the extremely traumatized condition of the survivors, will not only pose a nightmare to the medical authorities, but to the nation, as a whole.

It is wishful thinking to believe that, the possibility of Nuclear Weapons being used, is remote even during War, given the horrendous experiences of *Hiroshima* and *Nagasaki*. However, it is best to be optimistic about this issue, because complete protection from a modern day Nuclear Holocaust, will remain on paper only, though some preparations like underground shelters etc. may be created, as has been done in many advanced countries. It is therefore fair to believe that, planning for the mitigation of Nuclear Disasters of the magnitude they are likely to be, may be futile, and not cost effective. A pragmatic approach would be, to prepare for Radiological Disasters, since the use of Radiological Bombs or Devices, in the present day security environment, cannot be ruled out. For instance a Security Alert has been sounded recently, in the USA, regarding four persons, believed to be planning to explode a Radiological Bomb. Radiological Disasters, which are more likely to occur, have most of the characteristics of Nuclear Disasters, though of much lower magnitude. It is possible to be prepared to mitigate such disasters through awareness programmes, training, equipping the rescue parties with NBC protective equipment, providing the hospitals with necessary medicines, equipment, etc. Therefore, to begin with, preparation for Radiological Diasters should be taken up with full earnest, both at the national, and the district level.

6

Management of Biological Disasters

Biological disasters can be caused by overt or surreptitious use of living organisms or their toxic products to cause disability and death to men, animals and crops. Little is known about masterminding this form of disaster deliberately, though most countries have active research programmes on the development of these living organisms and toxins. Due to the very high number of casualties which can be caused by biological agents, they are also termed as weapons of mass destruction.

Biological warfare has obscure antecedents, which go far back in history. Poisoning of wells is an old trick. In the 14th century, during the Battle of Crimea, bodies of plague victims were thrown over the fortress walls, forcing the abandonment of the fortress. By the 16th century, an Italian tactical manual described how to construct artillery shells for delivery of disease to the enemy. In the colonial days it is reported that European traders passed out blankets of small pox victims to Red Indians in North America to reduce their fighting strength.

In more recent times, agents are believed to have inoculated animals being shipped to Europe so that diseases would be carried there. They also infected Romanian cavalry horses.

Active programmes of biological warfare research were carried out in the warring countries of World War II, like USA, USSR, Japan, Germany etc. Limited biological warfare agents are reported to have been tested by Japan in China during World War II though no large scale use of biological warfare agents are known to have been attempted. However, use of biological agents in the future wars cannot be totally ruled out.

In times, other than war, biological disasters could take place due to the leakage of these organisms into the environment due to accident, animals being used for research could escape while being transported from one place to another, or the germs kept in the laboratory may be stolen by interested parties etc. However, such news is generally kept secret and may be revealed to the public long after the epidemic is brought under control or is over.

What would be of greater concern to us in the context of this book is the use of biological warfare agents by terrorists and non-state actors. Any laboratory with a modern scientific programme can produce effective biological agents. The initial capital investment may be slightly high due to the requirement of controlled conditions, but subsequently the agents are very inexpensive to produce. Research has now made it possible to produce new strains of living organisms with striking modification in virulence, antibiotic resistance and even identifying characteristics. In 1900, the first viral disease of human beings was discovered—"Yellow fever". Since then, there has been no let up of discovering new strains and viruses. Use of a biological agent is difficult to be proved because though the disease can spread quickly, most natural outbreaks move quite slowly and by the time the epidemic or disaster is realised, the proponents of the disaster would have moved far away.

Biological Weapons—Weapons of Choice

Biological weapons as WMD could well become the weapons of choice in the near future. The advantages of being cheap, easily produceable and concealable will become even more pronounced as advances in biotechnology continue. This could produce agents with revolutionary offensive capabilities for use against populated areas. Specific advantages of biological warfare agents for use by terrorists would be:

- extraordinarily small quantities provide extraordinary lethality.
- sophisticated delivery means are not required; even pocket size atomisers could be used.
- information on development and dissemination of agents is readily available from open sources.
- ease of concealment and delivery make both the biological agent and user difficult to detect and identify before and after use, complicating both defence and response.

Nuances of Biological Agents

Biological weapons can be manufactured with very little infrastructure and expertise. For instance, a beer factory can be used to manufacture biological weapons. Monitoring of bio-weapon facilities is an extremely difficult task. Could this have been one of the reasons why the Coalition Forces of USA and UK could not find any biological weapons in Iraq after the Gulf War? Some of the difficulties in handling the spread of biological weapons and contagious diseases are:

- Difficulty in monitoring activities related to biotechnology, since research and development activity is ongoing in laboratories of medicine factories, institutions teaching biology or biotechnology, research and development organisations etc. There is no registration of such facilities with any government body nor is there any government legislation to monitor them. Hence, such facilities could be misused by design or by default by interested parties.

- The common people in our country are not conscious of public hygiene and lack the awareness of threat due to biological agents.
- The public health system in our country is very poor; this is evident from the piles of garbage stacked in various areas, the clogging of the rainwater or sewage system, waterlogging in the streets due to rain etc. There have been instances where the sewage lines have got connected with the drinking water supply line. (In such situations, no terrorists are required to create a biological disaster.)
- Inadequate funding for study and analysis of biological agents and lack of an integrated and holistic system to deal with major epidemics / biological agent attack.

Prevention of Biological Disasters

The threat posed by biological weapons is real, growing and evolving rapidly with the pace of technology. Facilities and equipment used to produce biological agents for illicit purposes cannot be distinguished from their legitimate counterparts. Moreover, disease causing organisms are ubiquitous in nature and key equipment and agents suitable for their production are housed in various facilities around the country including private companies and universities.

The Biological and Toxin Weapons Convention (BTWC) has been in force since 1972. However, not much attention seems to have been paid to enact implementing measures.

National measures need to be adopted to identify the select list of agents and toxins that could lead to biological disasters and to ensure that dangerous pathogens and toxins are utilized only for prophylactic, protective or other peaceful purposes. It should be limited to authorised entities and persons responsible for the development, stockpiling, acquisition or retention of these pathogens. Such measures should not only involve government personnel and facilities but also those in the private sector and academia.

Enforcing the protective measures is as important (if not more) as tabulating them. Enforcing agencies should be armed with additional powers to take criminal and penal actions if deemed necessary, to avert the possibility of biological disasters.

Characteristics of Biological Disaster Agents

The most important characteristic of microorganisms is that they are living and their infectivity is defined as their ability to cause disease. The fewer the microorganisms required to give rise to the disease, the greater is the infectivity index. Some of the characteristics of these agents are as follows:

- A majority of agents employ germs, which are very small living organisms and which will only grow and reproduce under suitable conditions. They are mostly non-persistent, in that they are extremely susceptible to variations in temperature, humidity and sunlight and will therefore die off rapidly if disseminated in unsuitable conditions.
- Some agents such as "Anthrax" are very resistant to climatic effects and can be classified as persistent. Due to this characteristic, the agent is known to have been delivered even by post as has been seen in the USA in the recent past. However, Anthrax is not transmitted from person to person and one has to infect each person individually. A picture of a patient suffering from "Cutaneous Anthrax" is shown in Figure 6.1.

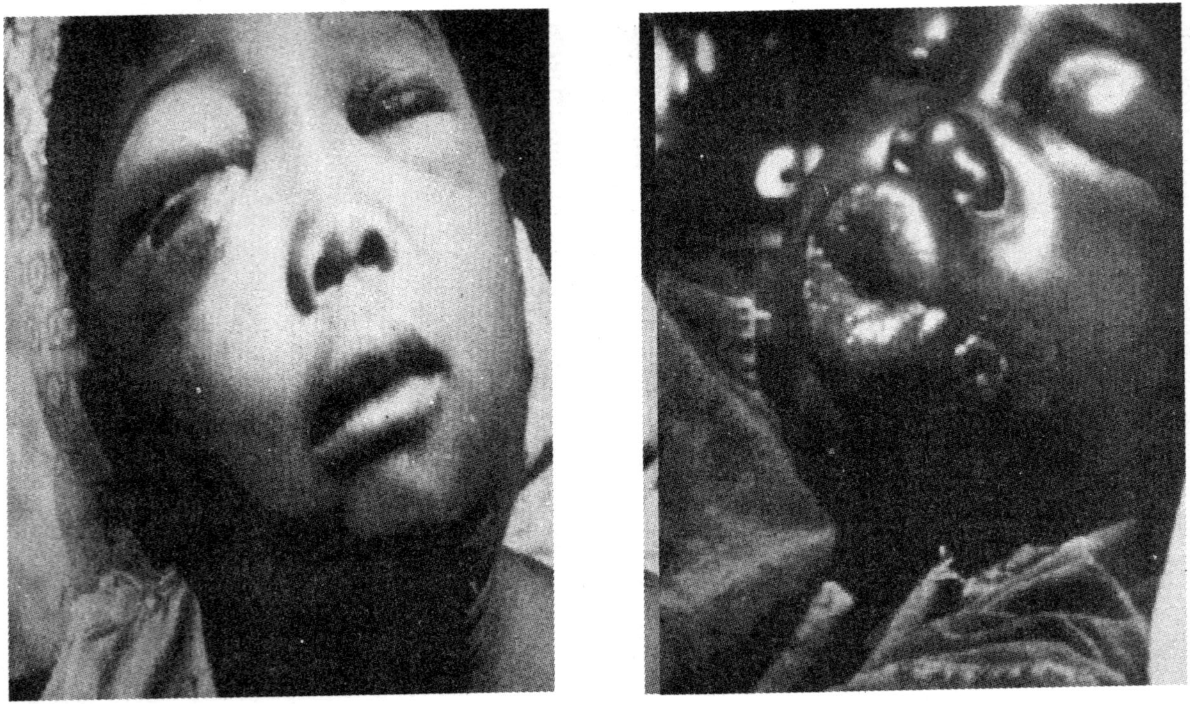

Fig 6.1 Effect of Cutaneous Anthrax

- The germs generally require an incubation period before the appearance of the disease. If the germ utilises the infected person as a carrier, then, before it is known, a large number of persons who come in contact with this person will be infected unknowingly and the disease will spread in geometric progression. For example, a disease like plague may cause an epidemic and a biological disaster.
- The agents can enter the human body through the skin and eyes, by eating contaminated food, drinking contaminated liquids and through the respiratory route, particularly if the agent has been dispersed in aerosol form.
- The most favourable conditions for employing biological agents is from an hour before sunset to an hour after sunrise. Moderately cool temperature and high moisture favour the survival of most biological agents. However, certain vectors may be less active during cool to cold temperatures, like insect-borne disease germs. Sunlight is very destructive for biological agents.

Biological Disaster Scenario

Unlike other disasters the destructive effect of biological warfare is not visible since the disaster takes place silently and over a period of time, and generally does not adhere to geographical boundaries. Was "SARS" a case of biological disaster? The world may come to know much later.... how long has the disease been dormant or in the incubation period? How did it start? Where did it originate? These are some questions which will remain unanswered. However, the effects have been seen by the world. The disease has travelled from country to country without its passage being detected, and in a short period of time claimed many lives worldwide.

Diagnosis of a Biological Agent

A thorough knowledge of the disease (which is the cause of biological disaster) against which protection is being sought is essential. One must know the proper antibiotic to use, its dosage and the correct schedule and time during the incubation period to administer the drug.

In the event of a biological attack, the rapid establishment of an accurate specific aetiologic diagnosis will be the all-important factor for medical management. In contrast to naturally occurring epidemics, in which the disease incidence builds up over a period of weeks or months, in an artificially induced epidemic the peak will occur within hours or within a few days.

Identification of commonly known biological warfare agents such as virus of small pox, can be accomplished within 1 to 2 hours. However, diagnosis of other diseases or identification of viruses may take four to six weeks during which the disease will spread further. From a practical point of view, one must assume that the terrorists/agents would employ organisms other than the ones commonly encountered in every-day medical practice. The symptoms and treatment of biological warfare agents and toxins are given in Appendices 'C' and 'D'.

Action by Various Agencies

The medical authorities of the district, state and possibly at the national level will have to lead the mitigation process. They will be responsible for identification of the agents and disease, the possible source of the disease, the prophylactic actions that are to be taken, the treatment that is to be rendered, the precautions that are to be adopted by the general public and the medical staff, so that the disease is not allowed to spread. The other agencies like Civil Defence, NGOs, Media and the local population will only be able to supplement the efforts of the medical agencies.

Medical Authorities: Once the illness begins to appear, the number of people affected, the time relationships, the similarity of the clinical picture, the sharply defined geographical boundaries, the existence or non-existence of any common source of exposure such as food or water etc. have to be studied and an epidemiological picture created.

- Detection of the virus as early as possible will be of paramount importance. For example, certain viruses can be identified within 4 to 12 hours using blood samples taken directly from the affected.
- Once the virus is detected all efforts have to be made to detect the antibody. The success or failure of medical mitigation will depend on the rapidity and accuracy of the diagnostic efforts.
- It is important that the medical personnel handling the casualties take proper precautions. The tendency of individuals in an emergency situation to become careless regarding food and water sanitation, general hygiene, and other disease control measures could produce detrimental effects.
- Ensuring that the hospitals prepare wards for isolation of patients and also have a separate reception system for accepting them. Patients standing in a line to be admitted along with general patients may lead to spread of the disease within the hospital itself.
- Since the spread of the disease will have no geographical barriers, all hospitals in the adjacent districts and states should also be prepared to receive the patients in their isolation wards.

Media: The media will have a very important role to play in case of a biological disaster. The first and foremost will be to broadcast information which is validated by responsible medical authorities. Broadcast of hearsay messages which may not be correct could lead to undesired panic. Some of the broadcast that could be done by the media in consultation with the medical authorities are:

- The preventive measures that should be taken to avoid spread of the epidemic.
- Inform the people of the early symptoms of the disease so that mitigation procedure can be commenced.
- Advise the people not to hide any cases of the disease since, it will be detrimental not only to the patient but to other members of the family as well.
- Advise the people to inform the medical authorities (telephone numbers to be broadcast) regarding any information of the disease that they may have.

Police: The source of the disaster has to be ascertained in order to bring to justice the culprits. However, the police may not be fully qualified to track the disease. It is recommended that specialists in the field be grouped with the police to ascertain the origin.

Civil Defence Organisations and NGOs: Civil defence organisations and NGOs are experienced in receiving and providing services to large and sudden number of displaced persons. But just how prepared are their frontline staff to deal with issues such as quarantine, barrier nursing, decontamination, even with the diagnosis of the clinical signs, is a question of alarm. Few, if any, health workers would have seen a case of anthrax or pneumonic plague, yet early recognition of it may be critical to the chance of stemming mass infection. Gathering together the correct combination of human resources to cope with the potential of mass anxiety of victims, who may not know whether they have been exposed or not, will also be a major challenge for these organisations.

Another important concern is how humanitarian workers themselves are to be protected while they are assessing the requirements or providing care and assistance to people fleeing from suspected areas of contamination. Therefore they should be detailed only for tasks like provision of food, clothing, guides for external assistance etc. However, it would be of great help if certain organisations are in a position to provide doctors or medically trained staff.

Civil Administration: Whether it is a Biological Disaster, or the spread of a disease or epidemic, the Civil Administration will have the greatest role to play. During the threat of Plague in Baroda, it was the Civil Administration, which probably displayed the greatest efficiency, and subsequently, Baroda was converted into the cleanest city in the country. It will be the duty of the Civil Administration to co-ordinate the services of all the players, who would be required to mitigate the Disaster. In order to be able to do the same, the Administration will have to be aware of the strengths and weaknesses of its area of responsibility. It will have to know the areas which are susceptible to the rapid spread of the epidemic, the capacity and facilities available in the hospitals, not only in their area of responsibility, but also in the neighbouring districts, the Para Medical personnel, who could be mustered up to mitigate the Disaster etc. The greater the preparedness of the Civil Administration, the quicker the Biological Disaster will be brought under control.

Conclusion

The emerging biotechnology of drug discovery and the rapid advance of knowledge about molecular biology promise great advances in medicine, biology, psychology and a host of related sciences. However, the same tools that are revolutionising drug discovery can be used to discover novel biochemical agents for the purpose of weaponisation. Related developments in chemistry and chemical engineering have similar results.

It is essential that a "Bio-terrorism Preparedness and Response Office" be formed at the National and State levels, with branches particularly in the major cities to help target areas for preparedness activities, including planning, improved surveillance and epidemiological capabilities, rapid laboratory diagnostics, enhanced communications, medical therapeutics, stockpiling etc. The Bio-terrorism Preparedness and Response Office could be a part of the National Disaster Management Authority, so that minimum additional infrastructure is required to be created or put in place to meet such situations may be put in place.

7

Preparing General Public for WMD Disasters

With the proliferation and easy availability of WMD, the study of defensive measures associated with Nuclear, Radiological, Biological and Chemical disasters has gained increased importance. Use of chemical weapons to cause disasters has assumed greater importance since these can be produced easily and are considered as poor man's bomb. Today, a biological, chemical or radiological threat of attack by terrorists is very real. It is not a matter of 'if' but rather 'when' a terrorist initiated chemical, radiological biological attack will take place. Terrorist groups are likely to utilise weapons of mass destruction, not only because of the high casualties at low cost, but also because of the panic and fear psychosis that it creates. The repeated checks and frisking of passengers at airports (particularly after the September 11 attack in New York) is a case in point of the effect of threat by terrorists.

The success of a terrorist attack will depend on the casualties it can cause. With the jehadis or suicide bombers having no requirement to escape, the disasters may be caused in less expected areas like inside temples, cinema halls etc. from where it will not be easy for the attacker to escape without getting affected. To score higher casualties, attacks will have to be in congested areas where the density of population is high. Attacks in larger cities are more likely than attacks in villages or smaller towns and cities, for drawing greater publicity. However, large gatherings in smaller places like the Kumbh Mela etc. could also be the intended targets for the terrorists. Though there is no way to predict where an attack will take place, and what will be its nature, people in general must prepare themselves so that damage from a WMD disaster can be minimised.

Would Preparation Lead to Panic

There is a possibility that publicity of such impending disasters may cause certain amount of panic among people. This should be accepted so that people are aware and do not panic when a disaster takes place. For example, in many a government transport system a cautionary notice is printed to check and report unclaimed packets and baggage, particularly under the seats. People have got used to the message and it does not cause panic, though most people make an effort to inspect below their seat and surroundings. After all, it is their life, which may be at peril. However, the preparatory and cautionary measures should be pragmatic, well packaged, publicised with maturity and easily implementable.

Awareness of the Characteristics of WMD

Nuclear or Radiological Threat. The effects of a nuclear or radiological explosion will be similar, though the magnitude of a nuclear explosion will be much larger than a radiological explosion. There are many similarities between the characteristics of a large conventional explosion and a nuclear explosion. The main difference that can be seen or sensed is the magnitude of the effect. The distinguishing characteristics of a nuclear explosion will be an intensely brilliant and blinding flash, a very intense wave of heat and an extremely powerful blast wave which will first move outwards from the scene of blast and then move inwards towards it, accompanied by very strong and gusting wind. If one is caught in the open when a nuclear device explodes one should immediately:

- Drop to the ground and face downwards with head in the direction of the blast.
- Close eyes and mouth.
- Protect ears with the thumb after covering the eyes with the palm.
- Keep hands under the body, if unprotected.
- Remain prone until all effects of the explosion have passed and the debris stops falling.
- Count till five. If one is alive one will survive.
- Move under cover/shelter or evacuate upwind of the suspected area.
- If inside buildings and the incident is outside, one must stay inside, turn off the air-conditioners and seal the windows and doors with plastic tape.

The blast will soon be followed by the falling to earth of radioactive dust known as nuclear fallout. It presents a hazard to personnel because of the harmful effects of radiation. Types of injuries that can be caused by radioactive fallout are:

- Serious internal injuries if the fallout is inhaled or ingested.
- Burns from radioactive dust on the skin.
- Internal injuries through radioactive particles entering the body through open wounds.
- Radiation sickness or illness sustained from radioactivity.

To reduce the effects of radioactive fallout, the body should be covered as far as possible. Since radioactivity cannot be destroyed, the clothing should be brushed of dirt, mud and dust and removed at the earliest opportunity. They should be packed in a polythene bag, if possible, and not left in the open lest contaminate others. At the earliest opportunity, one should decontaminate oneself by scrubbing and washing with soap and water. In case there are burn injuries the person should try and wet the area under running water to reduce the temperature and contain the burn.

In case of radiation threat due to a "dirty bomb", that is, use of common explosives to spread radioactive materials over a large area, the force of explosion and radioactive contamination will be more localised. While the blast will be immediately obvious, the presence of radiation will not be clearly defined until trained personnel with specialised equipment reach the scene. As with any other radiation one should try to reduce the exposure by:

- **Shielding:** Getting behind a thick structure. This will ensure that the radiation will be absorbed to a large extent and exposure to radiation will be minimised. The degree of exposure will depend upon the thickness of the shield.
- **Distance:** The farther one is away from the blast and fallout the lesser is the exposure.
- **Time**: Minimising the time spent in the area will also reduce the quantum of exposure.

Chemical Threat: A chemical attack is the deliberate release of a toxic agent in liquid, solid, aerosol or vapour form that poisons the environment. Casualties are caused by the toxic vapour entering the human body in any of the following ways:

- Inhalation of vapour through the respiratory tract.
- Ingestion of contaminated food and water.
- Absorption through the skin.

Possible indications of a chemical threat could be unexplained odour, a number of people suffering from pin-pointed pupils, watery eyes, twitching, choking, having trouble in breathing, dimness of vision, headache, running nose, intense salivation or losing coordination. Many sick or dead birds, fish and small animals or disappearance of insect life, could also be a cause of suspicion. The precautions that should be taken to reduce the effect of the chemical attack are:

- Try to discern from where the chemical agent is released and take immediate action to get away. In case one cannot get out of the area then one should try and rush to a shelter.
- If the chemical is inside a building, then one should get out of the building without passing through the contaminated area, if possible.
- Close the eyes and control breathing.
- Get under cover. If cover is not available and only vapour contamination is present, then one should lie on the ground as the toxic cloud generally forms 30 cm above the surface.
- Items like plastic sheets, raincoats etc. may be used to cover the body to avoid liquid contamination.
- Cover the exposed parts of the body with cloth. Use a wet cloth or towel on the face to cover the eyes and nose.

- Do not eat, drink or smoke in the contaminated environment.
- Sand, loose soil (obtained after removing 15 cm of possibly contaminated soil) or dry flour can be scrubbed on the exposed parts of the body or the contaminated parts to ensure that liquid contamination gets absorbed.
- Look for a source of water and wash the exposed parts of the body particularly the eyes and the face thoroughly with soap and water, being certain not to scrub the chemical into the skin. At the earliest opportunity take off all clothes, put them in a packet for subsequent disposal, and wash the whole body thoroughly with soap and water, for at least 15 to 20 minutes.

Biological Threat: A biological attack is the deliberate or accidental release of germs or other biological agents which cause disease or death in humans, animals or plants. Unlike an explosion, a biological attack may or may not be immediately obvious. The indicators of a biological attack could be:

- Unscheduled and unusual spray being disseminated.
- Abandoned spray devices.
- Sudden appearance of cases of unexplained disease/ death.
- Disease resistant to standard treatment.
- Large epidemic.
- Disease unusual for that area.
- Swarm of people seeking emergency medical attention.

It may however be possible to see signs of biological attack at times e.g. case of anthrax mailing in USA. Awareness of the biological attack will be in most cases through radio and television broadcasts. In the event of a biological attack, public health officials may not immediately be able to provide information on what to do, since it will take some time to determine what the illness is, how it should be treated and who is in danger. However, they should publicise through the radio, television, newspapers and internet the following:

- The signs and symptoms of the disease.
- The areas that are affected.
- Precautions that should be taken.
- Medications or vaccines available and being distributed.
- Where are they available? Where one should seek emergency medical assistance if one falls sick?

At the time of a declared biological emergency, if a family member becomes sick, it is important to be suspicious and seek medical assistance. Use of common sense, practise of good hygiene and cleanliness will avoid spreading of the germs. An extremely simple way of causing a biological disaster is to poison the water source of the area. More often than not the water tanks of the area are isolated with little or no fencing or protection. As a civic work, security and protection of these water sources must be undertaken since they could be easy sources of biological contamination. In addition, the people in the area should be conscious of this vulnerability and report of any suspicious movements seen in the vicinity of these places.

Home Preparations to Mitigate WMD Disasters

Keeping the security environment of the country in view, where radiological, biological or chemical attacks by terrorists is a definite possibility, it would be worthwhile if certain material preparedness is carried out by the public particularly in the large cities, for disaster mitigation. Some of these could be:

- **Storage of Food**: Simple items like rice, flour, lentil and salt can be kept in sealed plastic packets and turned over every month with fresh stocks. The more affluent can add ready-to-eat canned meat, fruits and vegetables, canned juices etc. There should be a stock of food duly sealed, available as reserve for the family for at least a week.

- **Storage of Water:** Water is an essential commodity for drinking and sanitation, particularly during the summer months. It will be difficult to store large quantities of water. However, at least three-day supply of drinking water for the family must be kept at all times in sealed bottles, at the scale of at least two to three litres per person. In addition, water should be preserved in large covered plastic buckets, for cooking and sanitation purposes. The bucket covers should be sealed with plastic tape the moment news of an attack is known.

- **Nose and Mouth Protection:** Face masks or dense-weave cotton material, that snugly cover the mouth and nose should be available for all members of the family.

- **Shelter in Place:** Staying put in the house would require creating a barrier from the potentially contaminated air outside, for survival. Plastic sheeting and tapes could be used to seal the doors, windows and air vents, if the room is to be sealed off from outside contamination.

- **Miscellaneous Items:** Emergency packs could be made—having first aid box containing commonly required medicines and miscellaneous items like scissors, screw drivers, tin and bottle openers, torch light with extra batteries, battery powered radio with extra batteries (to cater for contingencies of electricity breakdown) plastic garbage bags, whistle to signal for help, small hand towels etc.

There could also be a contingency where the house is too close to the disaster area and it is necessary to move to places further away. The movement will have to be done very quickly to be effective. For immediate departure it would be worthwhile to keep a suitcase or two ready with the following items. The emergency packs discussed (under miscellaneous items) could also be carried.

- Bed covers.
- Warm clothing (if required).
- Change of clothes and under clothing
- Spare shoes.
- Blankets.

Important documents like insurance policies, bank chequebooks and passbooks, should be kept in a waterproof packet to be taken along while evacuating the house.

Conclusion

The most pressing problem involving release of a chemical or biological agent by terrorists is that of its identification. It is only after the agent has been identified that neutralisation plans can be formulated, decontamination procedures adopted, emergency medical treatment plans made and environmental preservation precautions taken. The most serious consideration in this regard is that most civilian emergency service agencies, including specialised hazardous materials teams, do not possess the testing equipment to help identify sophisticated chemical or biological warfare agents that might be used in a potential terrorist attack. Therefore, in the present security environment in the country where a radiological, biological or chemical disaster cannot be wished away, it is essential that there is awareness among the general public, particularly in the metropolitan cities, so that casualties can be minimised and such disasters mitigated instead of leading to panic.

8

Preparing Hospitals for WMD Disasters

The main characteristics of casualties due to WMD disaster, which differentiates them from other disasters, is that, they are likely to be contaminated with radiological, chemical or biological agents/residue. Therefore, to treat casualties due to WMD disasters, hospitals must be geared up to decontaminate the casualties before they can be provided any serious medical assistance.

Nature of Casualties

In the case of a nuclear or radiological disaster the casualties are likely to be due to burns of varied degrees, physical injuries due to blast as also due to nuclear radiations. In fact the possibility of a casualty taking the brunt of more than one of these is fairly high. In addition, there could be eye injuries and retinal burns due to flash effect of the explosion. The treatment of the effects due to exposure to nuclear weapons will follow the conventional methods except in the case of injuries with concomitant contamination, which would merit decontamination. The other aspects of nuclear weapon casualties like the large number of burns and delayed cellular effects of radiation will require to be treated in specialised departments like marrow centres, malignant disease treatment centres, trauma centres, haematology centres, gastro-enterology centres etc.

The nature of casualties exposed to chemical warfare agents depends on the type of agent to which they are exposed e.g. nerve agent, blister agent, blood agent, choking agent etc. Decontamination of such casualties is a must in case persistent agents have been used. In case of non-persistent agents also, decontamination is essential; however, the importance is not as great as for persistent agents and it will depend upon the intensity of the agent and the duration of exposure. Treatment of the casualties will follow conventional methods. However, the specific antidotes have to be catered for because they are not likely to be available in sufficient quantities in the hospitals.

Medical problems associated with a biological disaster would require medical management on a mass basis rather than the administration of individual care. The major problems of medical care due to a biological attack or disaster would be those related to the large number of casualties. However, the casualties will be geographically dispersed and therefore special measures like decontamination facilities will have to be created in all hospitals. The agents / diseases, symptoms and treatment have been summarised in Appendices 'A', 'C' and 'D'.

Infrastructure Required in Hospitals

Every hospital whether private or government must have a Disaster Management Plan. Some government hospitals do have such plans (even if only on paper) but those are only for management of natural disasters or calamities. Since the casualties in case of WMD disasters are likely to be very high, the services of all hospitals in the area and beyond including private hospitals may be required.

Hospitals will not be identical as far as their layout and design is concerned; however, some features common to all hospitals are the reception area, areas earmarked for parking vehicles, emergency reception centre, outdoor patients complex etc. Although the treatment of WMD casualties follows conventional methods and standard treatment protocols, however, due to the peculiar nature of these casualties a decontamination zone is essential, which is generally not catered for in normal hospitals.

The hospital should be demarcated into two areas, viz., clean area and contaminated area. A prominent line should be drawn using paint or with tape, to demarcate the two areas. The closed or covered area of the hospital may be treated as Clean Area and the open area in front of the casualty department (generally the area for parking cars) could be earmarked as the Contaminated Area or any other suitable area, preferably in the downwind direction and away from the main hospital building.

Contaminated Area

Demarcation of contaminated area helps in segregating the contaminated personnel and prevents secondary contamination of hospital personnel and equipment. A prominent line, say a broad yellow line could clearly demarcate this area from the Clean Area. Casualties should not be allowed to cross the yellow line till they are decontaminated. The contaminated area should be established downwind so that the NBC contamination moves away from the hospital. Within the constraints, it should be possible to relocate the contaminated area in and around the hospital in case there is an appreciable change in the wind direction. The contaminated area should have the following facilities:

- Ambulance Parking Site.
- Casualty Reception Centre.
- Regulation Site.

- Intubation Site.
- Decontamination Site.

Ambulance Parking Site

The ambulances bringing the casualties will themselves be contaminated since they are coming from the disaster area. The vehicle driver and medical assistants accompanying the casualties should therefore be in protective gear. The casualties should be in casualty bags or wrapped up in polythene sheets as far as possible. This will reduce the chances of spread of contamination. The ambulances after unloading the casualties should move back to the disaster site without any delay. Earmarked personnel in protective gear should carry the casualties to the Casualty Reception Centre. This could also be done by civil defence personnel and personnel from NGOs to relieve the medical personnel for other duties.

Casualty Reception Centre

A Reception Centre has to be established away from the hospital complex. The casualties evacuated from the site of disaster should be brought to the reception centre directly or from the Ambulance Parking Site. Here the identification and documentation of the casualties will be done as well as their photographs taken (the photographs will be displayed in the Public Information Centre as discussed later in the chapter). Identification cards would have been tied to the wrist of the individuals during Triage at the disaster site. This should be checked and if not done should be ensured, as far as possible. Triage will once again be carried out at this place by the doctors based on the clinical condition of the patients and the casualties suitably delineated by means of colour discs as per the disaster management plan of the hospital. The broad parameters/guidelines for classification of casualties could be as follows:

Colour Code	Type of Casualties
Red	Casualties having severe conventional injuries associated with contaminated wounds and requiring urgent major surgeries.
Yellow	Serious radiological or chemical casualties having no conventional injuries.
Green	Casualties requiring mechanical ventilation.
Black	Very serious casualties with no chance of survival.

Table 8.1 Guidelines for Classification of Casualties.

Some of the very serious casualties may succumb to their injuries by the time they reach the hospital. Such casualties should be officially declared dead by the medical officer and documented with the issue of death certificate. This will assist in the family of the person to claim financial assistance, compensation and processing of life insurance claims etc.

Civil defence organisations and NGOs must assist the hospital authorities to maintain the Reception Centre so that the limited medical staff can be utilised for medical duties elsewhere. All personnel in the Reception Centre must be in NBC protective gear. If possible the records at this centre must be computerised.

Regulation Site

This is to be established close to the decontamination site and is brought into use when the decontamination site is overloaded and unable to accept any further casualties. Casualties brought here will be administered only initial treatment till they can be transferred to the decontamination site. The personnel at the regulation site should be in protective gear.

Intubation Site

Assisted medical ventilation may have to be undertaken for critical cases where the severity of the injury demands prompt intubation, even without the casualty being subjected to decontamination. Medical personnel will have to provide the intubation and therefore have to be in protective gear.

Decontamination Site

The casualties will be brought to the decontamination site from the Casualty Reception Centre or the Regulation Site. The aim of decontamination is to rapidly and effectively render harmless or remove poisonous substance from the casualties. Decontamination is defined as the reduction or removal of chemical, radiological or biological agents so that the casualties are no longer medical hazards. Agents may be removed by physical means or neutralized chemically. Decontamination of eyes, skin and wounds must be done. The process of decontamination for different contaminates will vary to some extent.

- **Radiological Decontamination**: Radiologically contaminated casualties are the ones whose outer body surfaces have been contaminated with fallout from nuclear detonation. These fallout residues in the form of dust, ash, dirt or mud, will adhere loosely to the clothing and skin of the patient. Once these residues have been removed, the patient no longer presents a radiation hazard, though he may require treatment for ingesting radioactive dust etc. Ninety to ninety-five per cent of the radiological decontamination can be accomplished by simply removing the outer clothing. The contaminated clothing ønce removed should be placed in bags, tagged and removed to a remote place for subsequent disposal. The second phase of the decontamination consists of washing or wiping the patient's face, hands and exposed parts with soap and water. This should get the person ninety-eight per cent decontaminated. The third phase consists of washing or clipping the hair and scrubbing the scalp with soap and water. There will therefore be a necessity of having spare clothes, soap and water at the decontamination site. Arrangements for a shower bath at the decontamination site will be ideal. Requirements of a shower bath have been discussed later in the chapter under "preparation of the wet decontamination site."

- **Biological Agent Decontamination:** Decontamination of persons contaminated by biological agents is not of very great concern since most of these agents are not dermally active (tricothenes mycotoxin being an exception). However, decontamination remains an effective way to decrease the spread of infection from potential secondary aerosolisation. Biological warfare agents can be decontaminated by chemical and physical methods. For chemical decontamination disinfectants, soap and water are used. It is important to use a brush with the soap to ensure mechanical loosening from the skin surface structures followed by rinsing with water. This method is often sufficient to prevent contact infection. The contaminated areas should then be washed with 0.5 per cent hypochlorite solution with a contact time of 10 to 15 minutes. This solution should not be used in the eyes, abdominal cavities or on nerve tissues. It will neutralize and render any non-hazardous biological agent within approximately 5 minutes. Physical decontamination is done essentially for clothing and equipment wherein the contaminated items are subjected to dry heat at 160°C for 2 hours or with steam at 121°C for 20 minutes at 1 atmosphere of over pressure.

- **Chemical Agent Decontamination**: This is done in three phases, namely, initial, dry and wet decontamination. During initial decontamination the bandages are removed and the wounds are flushed. The bandages are replaced only if bleeding recurs. Tourniquets are replaced with clean tourniquets and the sites of the original tourniquet decontaminated. For dry decontamination the casualties are completely undressed and the contaminated clothes are placed in numbered plastic bags. The same identification numbers could be written on the identification cards of the patients and medical case file. Dry decontamination is carried out with Fuller's earth for at least two minutes. The complete body surface except the eyes and exposed wounds should be subjected to dry decontamination. After undergoing dry decontamination the casualties are subjected to wet decontamination. In this the casualty is asked to take a shower bath and thoroughly scrub the body surface with soap and 0.5% hypochlorite or mild alkalis followed by a clean shower. The contaminated persons should undergo wet decontamination for a minimum duration of 4 to 6 minutes. Serious casualties may require assistance for wet decontamination. Medical staff both male and female should be available for this task. It must be ensured that the decontamination duration and quality are strictly adhered to, since even a drop of chemical agent may be fatal. Persons working in the wet decontamination area should be provided with disposable impermeable waterproof decontamination suits. The other personnel could be in NBC protective gear. Adequate replacement clothing, towels etc. should be available at the wet decontamination site for the casualties undergoing decontamination. From the Decontamination site the persons will proceed to the Clean Area of the hospital.

Clean Area

As has been discussed earlier in this chapter, the Clean Area will be demarcated from the contaminated area by a prominently painted yellow line. Essentially, the hospital or portion of the hospital premises will be the clean area. In the clean area the medical staff and assistants from civil defence organisations and NGOs are not required to be in protective gear so that thorough examination and effective medical management can be facilitated. In view of the different requirements of treatment for different casualties the hospital wards should also be demarcated according to the type of casualties.

- **Mild Casualty Ward**: Any conventional ward of the hospital adequately staffed and stocked would suffice for being designated as Mild Casualty Ward. However, the staff should know the sources and measures for obtaining specific antidotes.
- **Moderate Casualty Ward**: Provision of the specific antidotes should be catered for in addition to the facilities available in a conventional acute ward of a hospital.

- **Severe Casualty Ward**: Enhanced staffing and provisioning of adequate life saving and monitoring systems would be required. Preferably the Intensive Care Unit (ICU) of the hospital could be designated as the severe casualty ward.
- **Combined Casualty Ward**: Combined casualties i.e. moderate to severe conventional injuries associated with contaminated wounds may have to be taken up for emergency management without undertaking the decontamination drill. It implies that these casualties will be allowed to cross the yellow line without undergoing decontamination and therefore will be a contamination hazard inside the clean area. To cater for this contingency it is imperative that the combined casualty ward is located in a separate building, to lessen the chances of breakthrough of sanctity of the clean area. The staff in this ward would be required to wear double surgical gloves (for safety) and face masks to ensure protection from contamination. The medical and paramedical staff manning this ward should be well trained and knowledgeable of the specifications of confirmed treatment protocol against various types of agents.

Counselling Site

There will be a large number of patients suffering from extreme emotional stress as a consequence of being exposed to radiological, chemical or biological agents. In addition, many persons are likely to be traumatised by the often violent method in which their near and dear ones have succumbed to the effect of the agents or physical injuries or both. A psychological counselling site will therefore be very essential and should be manned by psychiatrists and counsellors. NGOs could play an active role in mitigating the trauma of such persons.

Public Information Centre

As the initial wave of a disaster wanes, people will flood the concerned government institutions with queries about the whereabouts of their near and dear ones. In the earlier chapters it has been discussed that identification of casualties should be done before transporting them to hospitals and crematorium. In addition, at each stage photographs should be taken of the casualties, particularly the unidentified persons. While the broadcast of names and identification is made via the radio, photographs could also be shown on the television. The hospitals to which a particular casualty has been evacuated could also be broadcast. This will help to reduce the mental stress and strain of the people to locate their near and dear ones. Similarly, photographs should be taken in the Reception Centre of the hospital (with their identification if possible) and put up on notice boards. Information regarding the severity of the casualty and his/her present state could also be maintained (if possible computerized) so that the visitors could be informed, and panic and uncertainty reduced.

Preparation of the Wet Decontamination Site

The casualties will use the wet decontamination site to take a shower and decontaminate themselves. Since the bathrooms of a hospital are generally inside the hospital premises, that are in the clean area, separate temporary shelters will have to be erected in the contaminated area for decontamination. It should be made in two portions; separate enclosures should be made for men and women. Minimally the structure could be of galvanized iron pipes with plastic screens on the sides. Showers should be fitted on top of each cubicle. The cubicles should be so organised that the persons decontaminating themselves can pick up the clean clothes easily from inside. Arrangements should be made to connect these shower cubicles with the existing water supply system of the hospital. Arrangements should also be made to place the packets of contaminated clothes duly tagged for subsequent disposal. The most important aspect of this wet decontamination site is that the contaminated water should not be permitted to go into the existing sewage system. Therefore, soakage pits should be dug and the contaminated water made to flow into it. In fact, it would be ideal if soakage pit for wet decontamination and water connection to the shower baths could be made a permanent infrastructure of the hospital. The shower shelters in prefabricated condition could be kept in the hospital to be assembled when required. A suggested pre-fabricated wet decontamination structure is shown in Figure 8.1.

Fig 8.1 A Pre-Fabricated Structure for Wet Decontamination.

Summary of Recommendations

The management of casualties after a WMD disaster will be a nightmare for the administration particularly since the numbers will be very large and the risk of contaminating others will be high. In addition, some of the hospitals in the area may be affected by the disaster directly or indirectly and hence may not be usable. At the national, state and district level legislation should be passed and orders implemented to ensure that all existing hospitals, whether private or government, have disaster management plans drawn up, particularly for WMD disasters. Preparation for WMD disasters will also cater for natural disasters or man-made disasters, but the opposite may not be true. Some of the facilities that will be essential to be catered for depending upon the patient handling capacity of the hospital are as follows:

- Preparation of separate soakage pits for contaminated water.
- Modifying the existing water supply system to supply water to the showers in temporary shelters when erected.
- Fabricating temporary shelters and maintaining them for use in the event of a WMD disaster.
- Preparing a WMD disaster management plan to include special sites for management of casualties, delineation of medical wards for various types of casualties, catering for the requirement of various types of equipment and medicines, interaction with civil defence agencies and NGOs etc.
- Provision and stocking of Fuller's earth, hypochlorite solution, soap, scrubber, clothes, towels, non-permeable plastic/polythene bags with tags (for disposal of contaminated clothing), specific antidotes for chemical agents etc.

* Provision of non-permeable disposable decontamination suits and protective equipment to include face masks, respirators, canisters, gloves, over-boots. Approximately 10 sets of the equipment for a 100-bedded hospital should meet the immediate requirement. These could be supplemented subsequently.

Conclusion

WMD disasters will pose a major medical management problem to the authorities, particularly because of the very large number of contaminated casualties in a very short time frame. All medical treatment facilities should be prepared to maintain the normal medical and surgical facilities free from possible contamination and yet be able to provide proper care to contaminated casualties. Effective physical protection, timely medical treatment and appropriate deployment of hospital resources can minimise the number of casualties. To be able to achieve efficiency in the management of WMD casualties it is of paramount importance that periodic practices (properly monitored) are conducted in the hospitals, incorporating the aspects of segregating the contaminated and clean area, demarcation of the contaminated area into the various facilities required and setting up those facilities, nominating the wards of the hospitals which will receive the various types of casualties etc. In addition, training of the medical staff in donning the protective equipment and working with the same could be practised.

9

The Way Ahead

The threat of WMD terrorist attack looms menacingly in India given the present security situation seen in the global strategic context, particularly as a fallout of the US and UK coalition forces invasion of the Iraq. Did the USA diagnose 'a boil' and having tried to treat it, give rise 'to cancer'? As we have seen, the chances of nuclear attacks are low, though radiological attack is possible; biological attack is possible, but its effects will develop slowly and mitigation will be a slow and steady process. A chemical attack is the easiest to perpetrate and hence has the highest possibility, particularly because of the easily available constituents essential for such a task. Preparation for a chemical disaster perpetrated by terrorists would to a great extent cover the preparations required for other forms of WMD disasters, because its characteristics have the characteristics of the other forms of disasters embedded into it. For example, like the nuclear or radiological disaster, the casualties in case of a chemical disaster will be high, sudden and contaminated. Similarly biological disasters would also give rise to contaminated casualties whose numbers will grow in geometric progression as time passes unless checked effectively.

The basic difference of mitigation of WMD disasters as compared to natural disasters is the fact that WMD disasters carry with them danger of contamination, its spread and its after-effects. The present disaster management plans of some hospitals cater for sudden influx of casualties caused due to natural disasters; however, they are not geared up for casualties due to WMD disasters. During a workshop on WMD disaster management in a hospital I asked the participants (all doctors from various hospitals) "In how much time would a hospital be ready to take in chemical or nuclear attack casualties from the time the disaster occurs?" The first prompt reply was fifteen minutes, which started expanding to thirty minutes and reluctantly (thinking it would be termed as inefficiency) to sixty minutes. This is at a stage when the hospitals neither have arrangement for decontaminating the casualties nor have the NBC protective gears required by the medical staff. "The first doctor who diagnosed SARS died of the same disease." Imagine the havoc that an ambulance carrying casualties from a chemical disaster area can cause if it comes straight to the emergency reception of the hospital. The vehicle and the casualties will unknowingly contaminate not only the other patients nearby, but also the medical staff who are to treat them. To ensure that the "Way Ahead" is as smooth as possible, the actions recommended to be taken at various levels are summarised in the succeeding paragraphs.

Intelligence

The intelligence network of our country should be strengthened so that proper monitoring of undesirable elements can be carried out, and the vulnerable areas kept under vigil. The vigil should expand so as to include all the indubitable sources from where the components of WMD are most liable to fall into the hands of the terrorists. Industries dealing with hazardous materials or materials which could be the components for WMD, ought to be placed under a strict protocol for inspection and safeguard.

Information Database

A database should be created at the national level to collate the information required to mitigate WMD disasters. It should include the various organisations to be contacted, the locations where disaster relief materials are available, the locations of RRT and other trained manpower, the places where the special medicines required for treating WMD casualties are located etc. The information base so prepared should be percolated to all concerned and updated periodically.

Communication and Networking

The quicker the flow of information regarding the WMD disaster, the faster will be the possibility of taking action to commence mitigating the disaster. Preparation time of relief personnel in the case of WMD disasters will be greater than in the case of natural disasters, because of the inherent requirement of having protection against the contagious nature of the disaster. In a town or city the police have the best communication networking and therefore they should create redundancies so that WMD disasters are catered for.

Awareness

The first responders of WMD disasters will be the local population. Therefore, it is essential that they are aware of the nuances of WMD disasters and what immediate action they should take to protect themselves or reduce the effects of the poisonous agents. For example, the first action that one should take in case of a chemical attack is to cover one's face with a cloth (preferably wet), move away from the area, and wash the exposed areas at the earliest opportunity. The awareness programme should be formulated and implemented in a planned manner. Some of the suggested methods are as follows:

- Screening of simple, short duration documentary films to project the various aspects of WMD disasters and precautions to be taken and broadcast the same periodically through television.
- Broadcasting messages to make people aware of what they should do in case of a WMD attack.
- Conducting periodic lecture-cum-demonstrations on WMD disasters in schools and colleges. The advancement and availability of information technology in schools and colleges, could be leveraged by producing and showing instructional films on WMD disaster management, produced on compact discs (CD).
- Training in WMD disaster management must be made mandatory in the schedule of training for NCC cadets, Girl Guides, Home Guards, Civil Defence Personnel etc.

RRT

The RRT will be required to detect and neutralise the source of the disaster, at the earliest opportunity. The personnel in the RRT should be imparted regular training in WMD disaster management and be equipped with state of the art chemical and radiological detection equipment, protective gear etc. The RRT should have integral transport and be so located that they can be moved to the site of the disaster in the shortest possible time.

Media

The media, both print and electronic, has a very important role to play in preparing the people for a disaster, mitigation of the disaster, and follow-up of the disaster. Imaginative and innovative broadcasts have to be made to sensitise the people and yet not alarm them, both before and after the disaster has struck. For once, reporting the various facets of the disaster should be to assist people and not report for reporting sake. For example, repeatedly showing the site of the accident and state of the casualties will serve no purpose, whereas broadcasting requests for specific type of assistance, flashing of the photographs of unidentified persons etc. would assist in ameliorating the disaster. The aim of the broadcasts and publicity should be clear.

Police

The police will be the first "organised responder" in case of a WMD disaster. Therefore, the following actions at all police stations are very important:

- Formulation of SOP (to include the contact telephone numbers of the persons in civil administration, armed forces headquarters, fire department, district medical officer, hospitals) for reacting in case of WMD disasters.
- Training of the police force in operating in a contaminated environment.
- Provision of basic NBC protective equipment for the police personnel.
- Periodic simulative exercises to be carried out for the tasks likely to be entrusted to the police.
- Incentives to be offered for qualifying in NBC courses.

Fire Department

The fire department personnel are professionally experienced to mitigate disasters, particularly due to fire accidents. Additional training will be essential to operate in a chemical or nuclear contaminated environment. They should be provided with:

- NBC protective gears including non-permeable suits for use during decontamination.
- Detection and alarm equipment, both for chemical and radiological disasters.
- Prefabricated decontamination structures.
- Training to operate in a contaminated environment.

Armed Forces

In disasters of any kind the civil administration always looks up to the armed forces. The armed forces are trained to operate in an NBC environment during war. However, the scenario of a disaster in a civilian area is quite different from that of a battlefield. Besides, the specialised teams that the armed forces have may not be available during war. Therefore, the support in WMD disasters from the armed forces should not be taken for granted like in the case of other disasters, particularly if the country is at war. In case the WMD disaster is during peace time, the armed forces can be depended upon, to provide the lead and command and control to mitigate the WMD disaster.

Medical

The greatest load for disaster mitigation will be on the medical and para-medical personnel. The government as well as the private hospitals will have to be geared up, and the staff trained to handle the casualties due to a WMD disaster. Some of the measures recommended are:

- Preparing an SOP for the hospital for disaster management to include the management of casualties of WMD disasters. This will automatically take care of the casualties due to natural disasters; however, the reverse will not be true. The SOP should include interacting with Civil Defence Organisations and NGOs for assistance, particularly in non-medical but supporting activities.

- Conduct of awareness programmes, or making the staff to attend workshops, seminars or courses being conducted by other organisations or institutions like the armed forces.
- Refreshing the knowledge of the medical staff with the treatment of WMD casualties like nerve gas casualties, radiological casualties etc, which do not take place every day.

Civil Administration

The responsibility for mitigation of disasters is that of the Civil Administration. It is of paramount importance that the Civil Administration is aware of the nuances of WMD disaster and train its key personnel on the actions that should be taken to mitigate such disasters. Some of the suggestions for the Civil Administration are as follows:

- Prepare a detailed SOP for the district to handle WMD disasters.
- Train and equip RRT in the city or district.
- Coordinate with adjacent districts for mutual support in case of destruction of own infrastructure.
- The District Collector and other officers should take keen interest in acquainting themselves with the nuances of WMD disaster management.
- Conduct courses on WMD disaster management for key personnel of the administration.
- Build awareness among the local populace without causing alarm.

- Periodically conduct training exercises involving all departments like the civil police, fire fighting department, civil defence, medical department etc. to validate the SOP prepared.
- Make provision for the basic protection equipment required for operating in a contaminated environment.

Conclusion

Terrorism is on the increase the world over and the fact that it may graduate to the use of WMD cannot be wished away. Every day that passes without preparing to face WMD terrorism may bring us one day closer to it. USA with its programme of Homeland Security has been preparing in a concerted manner against any form of terrorism, particularly WMD terrorism. It has gone to the extent of monitoring ports in foreign countries from where ships may be coming to her ports possibly carrying WMD. Considering the present security situation in India, where the news of attacks by terrorists (particularly jehadis) is very frequent, it is imperative that this aspect of WMD terrorism is taken with all seriousness by the planners and decision-makers and pragmatic measures implemented.

Appendix A

Chemical Warfare Agents
Symptoms and Treatment

Nerve Agents

They are a group of highly toxic organophosphorus compounds and are classified as "G" and "V" agents. The principal agents in this group are GA (Tabun), GB (Sarin), GD (Soman) and VX.

Signs and Symptoms

- Miosis often pinpoint, usually equal rarely unequal, may be normal if exposure has been percutaneous (or by ingestion).
- Frontal pain especially on focussing or in bright light.
- Salivation, rhinorrhea, nausea, vomiting, abdominal cramps, flatulence and involuntary defecation.
- Tightness of chest, wheezing, bronchorrea, dyspnoea, cough.
- Weakness, twitching and fasciculation of skeletal muscles.
- Ataxia, convulsions, respiratory failure due to Cheyne Stokes respiration and unconsciousness.

Treatment

The main principles of therapy for nerve agent poisoning are assisted ventilation, cholinergic blockade with atropine, enzyme reactivation with oximes and benzodiazepines.

- Assisted ventilation with respirator or by positive pressure through portable resuscitator may be needed for many hours or days. General supportive care such as IV feeding, restoring electrolyte balance, treatment of shock and control of infection will also be required.
- In mild to moderate intoxication, 2 mg of atropine should be injected IM at 15 min intervals until signs of atropinisation occur. Atropinisation should be maintained for 24 hrs by IM injection of 1-2 mg of atropine at intervals of ½ to 4 hrs as required. In severe poisoning 4-6 mg of atropine should be injected by slow IV or IM. If signs of atropinisation do not appear, the injection of 2 mg of atropine should be given at intervals of 5-8 min until such signs are obtained. Signs of atropinisation are a heart rate of 90-100 heart beats per min and dry mouth and skin.
- Enzyme reactivation with oximes, namely, pralidoximine chloride or pralidoximine mesylate. In severe poisoning 1 gm of the oxime should be injected by slow IV or by IM route every hour upto a max of 4 gm. In mild poisoning, 4 gm can be given orally and in the event of continued absorption from skin area, oral dose may be continued beyond the four-hour period. The recommended dose of obidoxime is 3-5 mg/kg body weight and the dose should be given by slow IV injection of 150-250 mg for the average man. After the first

dose of atropine has been given and a satisfactory response has been obtained a further dose may be given once or twice at intervals of two hours. No beneficial effect is likely more than 14 hours after poisoning.

- Benzodiazepines are anxiolytics which have anti-convulsant action. Diazepam is the drug of choice and should be injected IM at 10 mg dose initially and further doses should be considered at intervals of 4 hrs depending on the patient's condition.
- The casualty should be removed from the toxic environment as soon as possible. All his clothing should be removed and his skin should be decontaminated with Fuller's earth or washed with soap and water. 0.5 per cent sodium hydrochloride can be used to decontaminate the patient. Medical attendants should wear respirator, non-permeable clothing, boots and gloves while working in a contaminated environment.

Vesicants (Blister Agents)

This group of chemical warfare agents consists of Mustard, Nitrogen Mustards, Lewisite and Halogented Oximes, of which mustard is the best known.

Signs and Symptoms

- **Skin:** The cutaneous syndrome can be divided into four phases i.e. latent period, erythema, vesication and necrosis. When the erythema appears, the skin acquires a red colour which is accompanied by intense itching. At high doses blister formation starts generally between 12 and 48 hrs after contact which usually ruptures giving way to a suppurating and necrotic wound.

- **Eyes:** Mustard acts insidiously on the eyes, the symptoms being lacrimation, intense pain, photophobia and blepharospasm. Conjunctivitis and corneal lesions are finally observed.
- **Respiratory Tract:** Nasal secretions, burning pain in the throat, hoarseness of voice, apnoea and pronounced dyspnoea.
- **Gastro-intestinal Tract:** Nausea, vomiting, pain, bloody diarrhoea and prostration.
- **Systemic Action:** Headache, nausea, vomiting, anaemia, epigastric pain, leucopoenia and anaemia.

Treatment

- Absorbing powders such as Fuller's earth and chemical inactivation using chlorinating compounds such as 0.5% sodium hypochlorite can reduce physical absorption. Small wounds are to be washed with clear water while serious wounds are to be decontaminated with hydrophilic gauze and satins.
- Local application of cooling preparations e.g. calamine lotion. Topical antibiotics and cortico steroids may be applied over blisters and covered with sterile vaseline gauze.
- The antidote for lewisite is dimercaprol or BAL (British Anti Lewisite). Maximum dosage of dimercaprol is 3 mg /kg IM repeated every 4 hrs during first 2 days, every 6 hrs on the third day and twice daily for the next 6 days. Side-effects include nausea, headaches, perspiration, trembling and transient rise in blood pressure. Dimercaprol ointment and ophthalmic ointment should be applied for skin and ophthalmic lesions.

- Eyes should be cleaned with analgesic solution or ointment to reduce pain (excluding cocaine which produces corneal sloughing) e.g. amethocaine hydrochloride 0.5%. To prevent infection treat with appropriate antibacterial preparations and instil one drop of 1% atropine.
- Atropine sulphate solution 2-3 times a day. Apply some sterile vaseline between the eyelids to prevent sticking. Don't cover the eyes with bandage. The use of local analgesic preparation may be augmented by oral or parenteral administration of analgesics.
- Respiratory tract mild injury with hoarseness and sore throat usually require no treatment. In severe cases treat as for bronchopneumonia.

Choking Agents

Chemical agents, which attack lung tissues causing pulmonary oedema, are classified as choking agents. The best known of these is phosgene. It is a non-persistent chemical agent and is colourless with suffocating odour reminiscent of mouldy hay. Phosgene effects if inhaled, but has no effects on the skin.

Signs and Symptoms

During or immediately after exposure to dangerous concentration of phosgene the following signs and symptoms may develop:

- Irritation of the eyes, throat and respiratory tract with lacrimation, coughing and choking.
- Feeling of tightness in the chest, nausea and vomiting are prominent features in early stages.

- A latent period of 30 minutes to 24 hours followed by appearance of more significant symptoms and signs which may be precipitated with exercise. Breathing thereafter becomes rapid, shallow and difficult. Cyanosis occurs.
- Increasing quantities of frothy white or yellowish fluid may be expectorated. Later, fluid may become pink tinged (signs of pulmonary oedema).
- Circulatory collapse with clammy skin, low blood pressure, rapid thready pulse and cardiac failure may occur.
- Eight per cent of fatal cases succumb within the first 48 hours of exposure. Late deaths can be attributable to bronchopneumonia.
- Another characteristic finding in phosgene attack is that an individual gets a feeling of choking, severe cough and watering of eyes immediately. These disappear quickly and the patient starts feeling well. But after an interval of 1-6 hrs depending upon the dose inhaled, all these symptoms reappear with greater intensity. In advanced stages, shock develops and the patient may die from cardiac failure or asphyxia.

Treatment

- If respiratory symptoms appear, oxygen should be given early, freely and continuously at 6-8 litres per minute through oro-nasal mask.
- Steroid treatment should be initiated within a very short time after exposure. Ten puffs of beclomethasone or betamethosone valerate aerosol, 50 mg metered dose should be inhaled at once. This should be followed by five puffs every hour for next 10 hrs and then one

puff hourly for the next 24 hrs or as long as necessary (5 days at least).

- Systemic betamethasone (20 mg IV injection) or equivalent repeated IV or IM every 6 hrs for at least 24 hrs. During the next 5 days, systemic therapy may be reduced under chest X-ray control.
- Antibiotic cover should be considered with these high doses of steroids. Codeine phosphate, 30-60- mg/ asthaline/ aminophyline tablets to suppress cough can be given symptomatically as required.
- Use of expectorants, barbiturates, analeptics, anti-histamines and atropine are contraindicated in phosgene poisoning. Return to normal activity must be gradual in all cases.

Blood Agents

Blood agents produce their effects by preventing body tissues from using the oxygen of the blood when inhaled. Hydrocyanic acid (AC) and cyanogen choloride (CK) are the important agents in this group. In liquid form, they can be absorbed by skin and mucosal surfaces also. Both the agents are non-persistent.

Signs and Symptoms

Inhaling blood agents may produce symptoms within seconds and death within a few minutes. Acute poisoning is characterised by headache, vertigo and nausea. Later giddiness, palpitation, dyspnoea, unconsciousness and convulsions occur. Cardiovascular collapse, respiratory arrest, convulsions followed by death is seen in severe cases.

Treatment

- Crush two ampoules of amyl nitrite and hold close to the nose after inserting into face piece of respirator. If symptoms persist, the treatment of two crushed ampoules should be repeated every 3 to 4 minutes until normal breathing returns or until 8 ampoules are used.

- 300 mg (20 ml of 1.5% solution in glucose/water) of dicobalt edetate should be given intravenously over a period of one minute followed by IV injection of sodium thiosulphate. It should be administered only if diagnosis is certain, as dicobalt edetate is toxic to kidney and causes hypotention.
- Dimethyl aminophenol hydrochloride (DMAP) is very effective owing to rapid formation of methaemoglobin. It is life saving but not curative. IV thiosulphate is the definitive cure. DMAP is given IM in doses of 250 mg per man. This must be followed by sodium thiosulphate. 10 ml IV injection of 3% sodium nitrite followed by 50 ml (upto 25 gm) of 50% sodium thiosulphate solution should be given IV immediately.
- Resort to artificial respiration if breathing becomes difficult or stops. Oxygen should be given if available, but amyl nitrite must not then be used.

Appendix B

NBC Equipment

Vendors and Cost

Respirator

Vendors

- M/s Joseph Leslie, Mumbai.
- M/s Univest Technologies Pvt. Ltd. Mumbai.
- M/s Vijay Sabre Safety Ltd. Mumbai.

Cost (less taxes) Rs. 1900

Canister

Vendors

- M/s Shakti Engineering Industries, Gwalior.
- M/s Joseph Leslie, Mumbai.
- M/s Filter Manufacturing Ind. Pvt. Ltd., Kolkata.
- M/s Vijay Sabre Safety Ltd, Mumbai.

Cost (less taxes) Rs. 404

Overboots

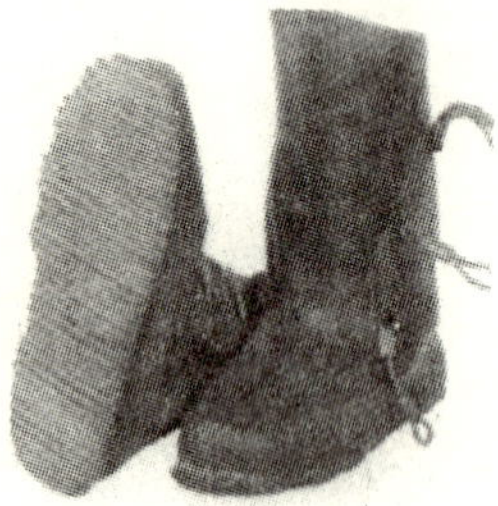

Vendors

- M/s Bengal Waterproof Ltd. Kolkata
- M/s Kumar Udyog, Kanpur.

Cost (less taxes) Rs. 800

Gloves

Vendors

- M/s Kapil Polymers, Kanpur
- M/s Calcutta Commercial Corp., New Delhi.
- M/s Indimech, Mumbai.

Cost (less taxes) Rs. 350

Non-Permeable Suit

Vendors

- M/s Bengal Waterproof Ltd., Kolkata

Cost (less taxes) Rs. 2560

Facelet Mask

Vendors

- M/s Joseph Leslie, Mumbai

Cost (less taxes) Rs. 184

Appendix C

Biological Warfare Agents

Symptoms and Treatment

Anthrax

It is a zoonotic disease caused by Bacillus Anthracis. There are two types of this disease, viz., cutaneous anthrax and inhalation anthrax. Cutaneous anthrax develops when the bacterial organism from infected animal tissues becomes deposited under the skin. The incubation period for cutaneous anthrax is one to seven days and without effective antibiotic treatment the mortality rate is 10-20 per cent. Inhalation anthrax develops when the bacterial organism is inhaled into the lungs. A biological warfare attack with anthrax spores delivered by aerosol would cause inhalation anthrax.

Signs and Symptoms

The disease begins after an incubation period of 1-7 days. Onset is gradual and non-specific with fever, malaise, fatigue in association with non-productive cough and mild chest discomfort. Initial symptoms are followed in 2-3 days by the abrupt development of severe respiratory distress with dyspnoea, diaphoresis, stridor and cyanosis. Physical findings may include evidence of pleural effusions, oedema of the chest wall and meningitis. Chest X-ray may reveal a dramatically widened mediastinum, often with pleural effusions, but typically without infiltrates. Shock and death usually follow within 24-36 hrs of respiratory distress onset.

Treatment

- Almost all cases of inhalation anthrax in which patients were treated after being symptomatic have been fatal, regardless of treatment. Historically, penicillin has been regarded as the treatment of choice with 2 MU given IV every 2 hrs. Tetracycline and erythromycin have been recommended in penicillin-sensitive cases. All naturally occurring strains tested to date have been sensitive to erythromycin, chloramphenicol, gentamycin and ciprofloxacin.
- Vaccines are available against some form of anthrax but their efficacy against abnormally high concentration of the bacteria is uncertain. Limited human data suggest that after completion of the first three doses of the recommended six-dose primary series with alum precipitated preparation of purified B anthrasis protective antigen (0,2,4 weeks and then 6,12,18 months), protection against both cutaneous and inhalation anthrax is provided.
- Prophylactic treatment with ciprofloxacin (500 mg BID) or doxycycline (100 mg BID) is recommended, to be continued for at least 4 weeks, should the attack be confirmed as anthrax.

Brucellosis

A disease caused by bacteria of the germs Brucella. It is a group of gram negative cocco bacillary organism, of which four species are pathogenic in humans. Brucella is highly infectious and it is estimated that inhalation of only 10 to 100 bacteria is sufficient to cause disease in humans. It has a long and variable incubation period (5-60 days) and low mortality rate.

Signs and Symptoms

It may occur as a non-specific febrile illness, which resembles influenza. Fluctuating fever, headache, myalgia, arthralgia, back pain, sweats, chills, generalised weakness and malaise are common complaints. Cough and pleuritic chest pain may occur in up to 20 % of patients. Gastrointestinal symptoms of anorexia, vomiting, nausea, diarrhoea and constipation, ileitis, colitis may occur in upto 70% of adult cases. Meningitis occurs in less than 5% of cases. Epididymo-orchitis may occur in humans as the most frequent genito-urinary form of brucellosis. Blood and bone marrow culture during the acute febrile phase will yield a positivity rate of 15-70 and 92% respectively. A dot-ELISA using an autoclaved extract of B-abortus has been found to be a sensitive and specific test for detection of Brucella antibodies.

Treatment

Isolation is not required other than contact isolation for draining lesions. The treatment recommended by the WHO for acute brucellosis in adults is doxycycline 200 mg/ day plus rifampicin 600-900 mg/ day for a minimum of six weeks. Ofloxacin 400 mg/ day and rifampicin 600 mg/ day is also an effective combination.

Plague

It is normally a zoonotic disease of rodents (e.g. rats, mice, ground squirrels etc) caused by Yersinia pestis. Flea, which live on the rodents can sometimes pass the bacteria to human beings, who then suffer from the bubonic form of plague. The pneumonic form of the disease would be viewed as the primary form after deliberate aerosol dissemination of the organism.

Signs and Symptoms

Normally plague appears in three forms in human beings' namely, bubonic, primary septicaemia and pneumonic. The buboes in the bubonic form are normally seen in the inguinal lymphnodes as the legs are the most common "flea bitten" part of the human body. Septicaemia is common, as greater than 80% of blood cultures are positive for the organism in bubonic plague. The pneumonic form causes infection of the lungs due to inhalation of the organism (primary pneumonic plague) or spread to the lungs from septicaemia (secondary pneumonic plague). In humans, the mortality of untreated bubonic plague is approx 50% whereas in pneumonic plague the mortality is 100 per cent. In bubonic plague the incubation period ranges from 2 to 10 days and the presentation is one of malaise, high fever, and one or more tender lymphnodes. Bubonic plague may progress spontaneously to the septicaemic form. After an incubation period varying from 2-3 days for primary pneumonic plague, onset is acute and often fulminant. The manifestations are malaise, high fever, chills, headache, myalgia, cough with production of bloody sputum and toxaemia.

Treatment

Standard precaution for healthcare workers exposed to bubonic plague and droplet precaution for those exposed to pneumonic plague until the patient has been on antibiotic therapy for at least 48 hrs is recommended. Streptomycin remains the drug of choice and is given 30 mg / kg /day (IM) in two divided doses for 10 days. IV doxycycline 200 mg initially followed by 100 mg every 12 hrs for 10-14 days is also effective. Gentamycin, ofloxacin and cipro floxacin are also effective. Prophylactic whole cell vaccine is available for use where the initial dose of 1.0 ml/IM is followed by 0.2 ml at 1 and 6 months. Three booster doses of 0.2 ml are given at 6 months intervals and then every 1-2 year.

Smallpox

Despite the global eradication of smallpox and continued availability of vaccines, the potential weaponisation of variola continues to pose a threat. Smallpox is caused by variola virus which occurs in at least two strains; variola major, and the milder disease variola minor.

Signs and Symptoms

Clinical manifestations begin acutely with malaise, fever, rigors, vomiting, headache and backache. Two to three days later lesions appear which quickly progress from maculae to papulae and eventually to pustular vesicles. Following eruptions on the lower extremities, the rash spreads centrally to the trunks over the next week. This centrifugal distribution is an important diagnostic feature. The usual method of diagnosis is demonstration of characteristic virions on electron microscopy of vesicular scraping. The development of polymerase chain reaction (PCR) diagnostic techniques promises more accurate and less cumbersome method of discriminating between variola and other orthopox viruses.

Treatment

- Antivirals for use against smallpox are under investigation. Cidofovir has been seen to have significant invitro and invivo activity in experimental animals. Droplet and air-borne precaution for minimum of 16-17 days following exposures for all persons in direct contact should be taken.

- Prophylactic vaccination after exposure to smallpox is effective in preventing disease if given within 7 days after exposure. A vesicle typically appears at the vaccination site 5-7 days post-inoculation, which forms a scab and gradually heals over the next 1-2 weeks. Side-effects include low fever and auxiliary lymphadenopthy. Passive immuno prophylaxis with vaccinia immune globulin in the dosage of 0.6 ml / kg IM is of value in post-exposure prophylaxis of small-pox when given within the first week of exposure.

Tularemia

Tularemia (also known as rabbit fever and deer fly fever) is a disease caused by Francisella tularensis. This organism can remain viable for weeks in water, soil, carcasses, and hides and for years in frozen rabbit meat. Transmission is by bites of infected deer flies, mosquitoes or ticks and after contact of skin and mucous membranes with tissues or body fluids or infected animals. After an incubation period varying from 1-21 days (average 3-5 days) onset is usually acute. In humans, as few as 10 to 50 organisms will cause disease if inhaled or injected intra-dermally. Tularemia may appear in several forms depending upon the route of inoculation, namely, ulceroglandular, glandular, typhoidal, occuloglandular, pharyngeal and pneumonic tularaemia.

Signs and Symptoms

Ulcero-glandular tularaemia (75-85 per cent of cases) is characterised by fever, chills, headache and malaise, and an ulcerated skin lesion and painful regional lymphadenopathy. Typhoidal tularaemia accounts for 5-15% of cases and manifests as fever, prostration and weight loss without lymphadenopathy. Respiratory symptoms, sub-sternal discomfort, and non-productive cough may also be present. Pneumonic tularemia is an illness characterised primarily by pneumonia and is seen in 30-80% and 10-15% of typhoidal and ulcero-glandular cases respectively. Treatment can be established retrospectively serologically. Fourfold rise in the tularemia tube agglutination or micro-agglutination titre is diagnostic of infection. Titres are usually negative in the first week of infection, positive in the second week in 50-70% of cases and reach max in 4-8 weeks.

Treatment

- Standard precautions are recommended for healthcare workers. Streptomycin (1gm every 12 hours IM for 10-14 days) is the treatment of choice. Gentamycin 3-5 mg/kg/day parentally for 10-14 days is also effective. Tetracycline and chloram phenicol treatment are effective as well, but are associated with significant relapse rates.
- Prophylactic treatment could be tetracycline 500 mg QID for 2 weeks given after exposure. A live, attenuated tularemia vaccine is available as an investigational new drug.

Q Fever

The endemic form of Q fever is zoonotic disease caused by **rickettsia**, **coxiella burnetii**. Its natural reservoirs are sheep, cattle and goats. Humans acquire the disease by inhalation of aerosol contaminated with the organism.

Signs and Symptoms

Following the usual incubation period of 2-14 days (average 7 days), Q fever generally occurs as a self-contained febrile illness lasting 2 days to 2 weeks. The disease generally presents as an acute non-differentiated febrile illness with headache, fatigue and myalgias as prominent symptoms. Pneumonia manifested by an abnormal chest X-ray occurs in half of all patients but only half of these will have cough or rales. Pleuritic chest pain occurs in about one-fourth of patients with Q fever pneumonia. Uncommon complications include chronic hepatitis, aseptic meningitis, encephalitis, osteomyelitis and endocarditis. Q fever is not a clinically distinct illness and may resemble a viral illness or other types of atypical pneumonia. The serological tests for Q fever include identification of antibody to C burnetii by indirect fluorescent antibody (IFA), ELISA and complement fixation.

Treatment

- Standard precautions are recommended for healthcare workers. Q fever is generally a self-containing illness even without treatment. Tetracycline (500 mg every 6 hours) or doxycycline (100 mg every 12 hours) for 5-7 days will shorten the duration of illness.
- Prophylactic treatment with tetracycline or doxycline during the incubation period can delay the onset of disease but not prevent the symptoms. An inactivated whole cell vaccine is effective in eliciting protection against exposure, which lasts for at least 5 years. Severe local reaction to this vaccine may be seen in those who already possess immunity.
- Person to person transmission is rare. Patients exposed to Q fever by aerosol do not present a risk for secondary contamination of re-aerosolisation of the organism. Decontamination is accomplished with soap and water or after a 30 minute contact time with 0.5% sodium hypochlorite or 70% ethyl alcohol.

Appendix D

Toxins

Symptoms and Treatment

Botulinum Toxins

The botulinum toxins are a group of seven related neuro-toxins produced by the bacillus clostridium botulinum. The bacillus "clostridium botulinum" mainly grows in poorly preserved food and has the inherent characteristic of poisoning minced pork, beef or other meat seasoned, preserved and encased in cylindrical skins, mainly to be eaten cold in slices or as a spread. These toxins, types A through G, could be delivered by aerosol over concentrations of human population. The clinical syndrome produced by one or more of these toxins is known as "botulism".

Signs and Symptoms

The onset of symptoms of inhalation botulism may vary from 24 to 36 hrs to several days following exposures. Bulbar palsies are prominent early, with eye symptoms such as blurred vision due to mydriasis, diplopia, ptosis, photophobia in addition to other bulbar signs such as dysarthria, dysphonia and dysphagia. Skeletal muscle paralysis follows, with a symmetrical, descending and progressive weakness, which may culminate abruptly in respiratory failure.

Treatment

- Botulinum attacks should be suspected if multiple casualties simultaneously show signs of progressive descending bulbar, muscular and respiratory weakness. Laboratory testing is generally not helpful in the diagnosis of botulism. Detection of toxin in serum or gastric contents is possible.
- Respiratory failure secondary to paralysis of respiratory muscles is the most serious complication and generally the cause of death. With tracheostomy or endotracheal intubation and ventilatory assistance, fatalities should be less than five per cent. Administration of hepta valent botulism antitoxin may prevent or decrease progression to respiratory failure and hasten recovery. Use of the antitoxin requires skin testing for horse serum sensitivity prior to administration. If no allergic symptoms are observed, the antitoxin is administered intravenously in a normal saline solution of 10 ml over 20 minutes.
- Prophylactic treatment could be provided by a pentavalent toxoid available under investigational new drug status which when given in the recommended primary series of 0, 2 and 12 weeks and then 1 year booster induces protective antibody levels in more than 90% of vaccines after 1 year.

Ricin

Ricin is a potent protein toxin derived from the beans of the castor plant (*Ricinus communis*) and is a potentially widely available toxin. When ingested, ricin causes severe gastrointestinal symptoms followed by vascular collapse and death. When inhaled as a small particle aerosol, it may produce pathologic changes within 8 hrs and severe respiratory symptoms followed by acute hypoxic respiratory failure in 36-72 hrs. Ricin can be produced relatively easily and inexpensively in large quantities in a fairly low technology setting.

Signs and Symptoms

The clinical picture in an intoxicated victim would depend on the route of exposure. Sublethal aerosol exposures are characterized by onset of fever, chest tightness, cough, dyspnoea, nausea and arthralgias in four to eight hours. Weakness, fever, cough and pulmonary oedema occur 18-24 hrs after inhalation exposure, followed by severe respiratory distress and death from hypoxemia in 36-72 hrs. Ingestion causes gastrointestinal haemorrhage with hepatic, splenic and renal necrosis. Signs and symptoms mentioned above when seen in large number of geographically clustered patients could suggest an exposure to aerosolized ricin. Laboratory findings are non-specific. Specific serum ELISA is available.

Treatment

- Patients with pulmonary intoxication are managed by appropriate treatment for pulmonary oedema and respiratory support as indicated. Gastrointestinal intoxication is best managed by vigorous gastric decontamination with super activated charcoal, followed by use of cathartics such as magnesium sulphate (Epson Salts).
- Prophylactic vaccine or prophylactic antitoxin is at present not available for human use. Use of the protective mask is currently the best protection against inhalation.
- Secondary aerosols should generally not be a danger to healthcare providers. Hypochlorite solution (0.1%

sodium hypochlorite) and/or soap and water can decontaminate skin surfaces. Calcium Oxychloride/ Calcium Oxide/Quicklime (bleaching agents or disinfectant) can also be used as decontaminants.

Bibliography

Army Medical Corps Centre and School, Seminar Papers, *Medical Response to NBC Warfare*, Lucknow, November 2002.

Centre for Counterproliferation Research, *The NBC Threat in 2005, Concepts and Strategies for Adversial Use of NBC Weapons*, National Defense University, 1997, USA.

Centre for Counterproliferation Research, *The Effects of Chemical and Biological Weapons on Operations*, National Defense University, Washington DC, May 2000.

Chacharkar, Dr. M.P., *Nuclear Disaster Scenario and Protection*, Defence Research Development Organisation, Defence Laboratory, Jodhpur, February 2003.

College of Military Engineering, Seminar Papers, *Seminar on Chemical Warfare*, Faculty of NBC Protection, Pune, April 1998.

Gander, T. J., *Jane's Protective Equipment*, Tenth Edition, 1997-98.

Gander, T. J., *Nuclear, Biological and Chemical Warfare*, Hippocrene Books, Inc, New York, 1987.

Grace, Charles, S., *Nuclear Weapons, Principles, Effects and Survivability*, Brassey's, 1994, UK.

Gripstad, Birger., *Biological Warfare Agents*, B.O. Rybeck, Stockholm, 1986.

Gripstad, Birger., *Chemical Warfare Agents*, Nils - Henrik Lundquist, 1983.

Institute of Nuclear Medicines and Allied Sciences, *Course Papers, 5th Training Course on Radiation Disaster Management*, New Delhi, March 2003.

Institute of Nuclear Medicines and Allied Sciences, *Course Papers, 6th Training Course on Radiation Disaster Management*, New Delhi, August 2003.

Miscellaneous articles from the Internet.

National Centre for Disaster Management, *National Disaster Management Plan, A Document Prepared by High Powered Committee on Disaster Management*, New Delhi, 2002.

National Centre for Disaster Management, *Report by the High Powered Committee on Disaster Management*, New Delhi, 2002.

Panicker, M.K.V. (Brig)., *Presentation Papers, Terrorism and Weapons of Mass Destruction: A Disaster Management Perspective*, Mumbai, May 2003.

Robinson, J.P. Perry, *Chemical and Biological Warfare Developments*, Stockholm International Peace Research Institute, Oxford University Press, New York, 1986.

Westing, Arthur, H., *Herbicides in War, The Long-term Ecological and Human Consequences*, Stockholm International Peace Research Institute, Taylor and Francis, London 1984.

Index

Notes

Notes

Notes

Notes